Scrappy Bits *appliqué*

Fast & Easy
Fusible Quilts

8 Projects

Foolproof Technique

stashBOOKS®
an imprint of C&T Publishing

Text copyright © 2014 by Shannon Brinkley

Photography and Artwork copyright © 2014 by C&T Publishing, Inc.

Publisher: Amy Marson

Creative Director: Gailen Runge

Art Director: Kristy Zacharias

Editors: Lynn Koolish and Deb Rowden

Technical Editors: Debbie Rodgers and Gailen Runge

Cover/Book Designer: April Mostek

Production Coordinator: Rue Flaherty

Production Editor: Joanna Burgarino

Illustrator: Kirstie L. Petterson

Photo Assistant: Mary Peyton Peppo

Style photography by Nissa Brehmer and instructional photography by Diane Pedersen, unless otherwise noted

Published by Stash Books, an imprint of C&T Publishing, Inc., P.O. Box 1456, Lafayette, CA 94549

Library of Congress Cataloging-in-Publication Data

Brinkley, Shannon, 1985-

 Scrappy bits appliqué : fast & easy fusible quilts - 8 projects - foolproof technique / Shannon Brinkley.

   pages cm

 ISBN 978-1-60705-880-9 (soft cover)

 1. Machine quilting--Patterns. 2. Machine appliqué--Patterns. I. Title.

 TT835.B7125 2014

 746.46--dc23

                    2013050339

Printed in China

10 9 8 7 6 5 4 3 2 1

Dedication

To Matthew.

Acknowledgments

A tremendous thank-you to my husband, Matt—without your unflinching support and encouragement, this book would not have been written. Thank you, Davin, for patiently occupying yourself with Legos and the like during my many hours of sewing and writing.

Thank you, Mom, from whom I inherited any artistic talent I have: You bought me my first sewing machine and supported, encouraged, and often commissioned the myriad of creative hobbies I've had over the years. It was your random idea to go to a quilt festival one year that started this whole thing. I love you.

I am hugely grateful to Stash Books and the whole C&T Publishing staff. Thank you especially to Lynn Koolish, Debbie Rodgers, Roxane Cerda, and everyone else who was involved in making this book a reality. Your suggestions, ideas, and direction made this book what it is. Thank you all so much. And thank you Kristy Zacharias and April Mostek for making this book so beautiful.

Thank you also to Timeless Treasures, Michael Miller Fabrics, Robert Kaufman Fabrics, The Warm Company, Prym Consumer USA, Pellon, and all the other companies who generously provided the incredible materials for the quilts in this book. It was a pleasure to work with your wonderful products.

Contents

Preface

Since I was a young girl, I have loved creating things with my hands—from the paper snowflake stand in my front yard to friendship bracelet club in first grade to my junior high dream catcher phase (the evidence of this phase is still all over my parents' house).

I began quilting and working with collage fiber art many years ago after visiting the International Quilt Festival in Houston, where I fell in love—wildly in love.

If you've been to the Quilt Festival, you know that it has an enormous quilt show, filled with beautiful, quilted perfection. As I was meandering through, stopping here and there for closer looks, I saw it—a large, breathtaking scene. It was a simple scene: a wooden chair in a garden, stream running below, fiery sun above, but I could not tear myself away from it. Looking closer, I noticed it was not pieced, but rather it was raw-edge appliquéd. My patient mother finally tore me away from it, but I could not get that quilt out of my head. It had more impact on me than any painting ever had—the textures; the incredible, vibrant colors; the movement the stitches created. I was smitten. Since then, fabric has been an obsession of mine: I love blending a variety of fabrics, vintage and new, with different colors, tones, and patterns, to create interesting and unique pieces. Sadly, I don't remember who the quilter was to thank her (or him) for the life-changing inspiration.

The modern quilt movement is an amazing thing. It has perpetuated this centuries-old tradition while making it relevant and accessible. Modern quilters, like modern artists, are constantly

pushing boundaries, breaking rules, and trying new things. I find it so exciting that raw-edge appliqué can be translated into the modern quilting realm, opening up many possibilities for the modern quiltmaker.

I love traditional piecing techniques. I love seeing a plan slowly unfolding and coming together on my design board. But piecing does take time, and I sometimes miss the instant gratification painters can get from slathering and dragging paint on a canvas—that immediate, tactile gratification. That is what I love most about the techniques in this book—taking gorgeous pieces of fabric (works of art in themselves) and moving them around to create an image or texture.

The other thing I love about this quiltmaking technique is that the quilts can be made as simple

or as complicated as you like. Maybe you have been interested in quilting for a while, but you are overwhelmed with all the different books and techniques out there and with the amount of time and precision you think quilting requires. Are you an artist looking for a new medium of expression? Have you been quilting for years and find yourself looking for another technique to add to your repertoire? Whether you are a professional sewist or one who just bought your first sewing machine, you can make the quilts in this book. If you can sew in a straight line, you can make the quilts in this book—some of them took me as little as eight hours to make! We'll go step by step through my simplified, efficient process, and by the end of the book, you will have all the tools you need to make one of the quilts in this book or create one of your own!

How To Use this book

The Basics

In the first part of this book, you'll learn about the raw-edge appliqué technique I call Scrappy Bits Appliqué—it's the perfect appliqué technique for modern quilters. You'll find several different options for each step, so that you will be able to modify and choose the techniques that best suit your preferences and design choices. You'll find out about these considerations and more:

- How to plan or design your quilt

- Color theory basics and how to choose a color palette for your quilt

- The materials needed and recommended for this style of quilting

- How to make the quilt, including different collage techniques and approaches as well as quiltmaking basics

- Several different methods for finishing a quilt

The Projects

In the second section of the book are eight quilt projects—you can put your new appliqué and collage quilting skills to work! Included are charts that will help you make each quilt in a variety of sizes as well as patterns for each collaged design.

For even more quilts and patterns, visit my website: thebottletree.net.

THE
BASICS

Planning your quilt

Some quiltmakers like to follow patterns, some like to completely design their own quilts, and some are in between—they like using patterns but always want to change things up a bit. No matter where you are in this quiltmaking spectrum, you can make a collage quilt.

Projects

For the eight projects in this book, you can use fabric and colors similar to those pictured or you can change up the colors and fabrics any way you like. Full-size patterns for the projects are included on the pattern pullout at the back of the book—they are ready to use to make the pictured quilts. Depending on the size quilt you are making, you may need to enlarge or reduce the patterns.

Creating a Design

If you want to create your own design and pattern, some of you may have no trouble drawing a design the exact size you need. If you don't want to draw your own large pattern or are creating a particularly complex design, I have some simple solutions for you! You can make your own full-size pattern using a copy service that does large-scale enlargements, or you can use graph paper and Tru-Grid material to scale the image to the needed size.

Tip *If you want to completely design your own quilt, use the information in this Basics chapter and refer to the Yardage Chart (page 102) to see how much fabric you'll need.*

Making Your Own Pattern

Either draw your own design or find a design you can print. If you search online for images, try using search terms such as *vector*, *outline*, or *printable* to find simple images that can easily be traced and cut out, and that will translate well into the collage medium. For example, images with a lot of depth and shadows may be difficult to replicate in a collage.

Important: If you are using a design that is not an original design that you made yourself, make sure that the design is copyright-free or get permission from the creator or owner of the design.

ENLARGING USING A COPY MACHINE

Materials needed: copy machine capable of enlarging images (copy shops often have machines capable of large-format printing)

After you have the drawing or printed design, use a copy machine to enlarge the image to the size you need.

ENLARGING USING A GRID

Materials needed: graph paper, Tru-Grid (see Resources, page 109)

1. Draw or trace the design onto graph paper. Be sure to have 1 square on the paper represent 1 square inch on your actual quilt. For example, for a quilt that is 50˝ × 60˝, the design on the graph paper should be 50 squares × 60 squares.

2. Enlarge the design by drawing the part of the design in each graph paper square in the corresponding square on the Tru-Grid.

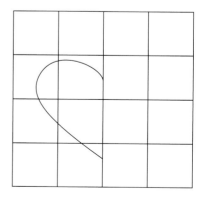
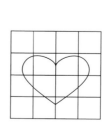

Choosing a Color Palette

Who doesn't love picking out colors? A color palette may be predetermined by a room's color scheme or the preference of the lucky person receiving the quilt you are making. If not, here are a few ideas to keep in mind.

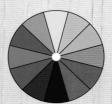 Consider the color wheel when choosing the predominant colors for a quilt. I use C&T Publishing's Ultimate 3-in-1 Color Tool to help me choose a palette, and I take it with me when buying fabric to ensure I choose the correct shades. For each of the 24 pure colors, the tool provides tints, shades, and tones, as well as 5 color plans.

Monochromatic

 *Monochromatic* means "one color." In this plan, the palette is based on one pure color; variety comes from choosing different tints, shades, and tones of that one color. Monochromatic color schemes are quiet and calm.

Analogous

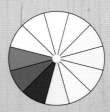 Choose one color and then select a few colors that are next to it on the color wheel. Analogous color schemes are easy to work with and the colors always work well together.

Complementary

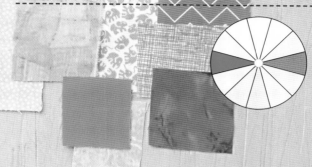

Complementary colors are colors opposite each other on the color wheel and are the boldest of color combinations. Placing complementary colors next to each other achieves the greatest level of contrast.

Tip *For a really dynamic palette, add one or two neutrals (white, black, gray, brown).*

Split-Complementary

This plan combines the previous two color plans. Select complementary colors and then choose one set of analogous colors to use as well. This color combination provides much of the contrast of a complementary color scheme but is toned down a bit.

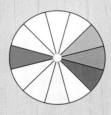

Triadic

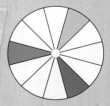

A triadic color plan uses three colors that are evenly spaced from one another on the color wheel. It provides contrast as well as balance and harmony.

Color Palette Ideas

Different color palette choices can completely change the look of a quilt. I usually choose the color(s) of my collage first. I typically prefer a monochromatic collaged image (page 12). After I've selected my collage color, I decide on the other colors needed—colors for the background, binding, and backing.

When choosing a background fabric (whether it is a solid piece of fabric behind the collage or a pieced background), decide whether you want the collage to stand out or to blend in with the background. If you want the collage to stand out, think about selecting a complementary color (page 13) or a neutral. If you'd like the collage to blend in, you may want to choose an analogous color (page 12).

After I've selected the collage and background colors (and usually after I've finished my quilt top), I choose the binding. When choosing the binding fabric, look at the quilt top and decide whether you want the binding to stand out, to blend in with and complement the quilt top, or to provide a strong frame for the design while not standing out too much.

I chose a split-complementary palette (page 13) for this quilt. The jade binding stands out but balances the bold and contrasting purple in the elephant. (See *Blocks for Elephants*, page 61.)

For this quilt, I chose a complementary palette (page 13) to use with the bold black and white neutrals. Since the border was so bold, I didn't want the binding to take away from that—I chose a print with a white background that had the same blue and orange shades as the center of the quilt. This brought those colors to the edge, allowing for a more balanced design. (See *Tamed Fox*, page 51.)

I wanted a very natural, organic look for this quilt. So I went with a monochromatic palette (page 12) with the neutral background. The brown binding closes in the quilt top, providing a strong frame for the design while not detracting from the main image. (See *Windy Poplar*, page 57.)

I choose the backing last since it is usually the least visible element of the quilt. Just because it is on the back, that doesn't mean it does not matter. The backing can make a strong statement about the rest of the quilt. Choosing a backing that really pops might be a great option if you've chosen a simple palette for the quilt top and binding—for this effect, choose a color on the opposite side of the wheel. If you'd like the backing to blend in and complement the rest of the quilt, choose a color already used in the quilt, a neutral, or an analogous color.

There are no hard-and-fast rules for color selection. If you'd like to break some of these color theory guidelines, go for it! This is your quilt—choose what looks good to your eye!

Choosing and

Materials and Supplies

Collage Fabric

I prefer using high-quality, 100% cotton fabric for my entire quilt, including the collage fabric. You can find this type of fabric at your local quilt shop, at most craft/fabric stores, and at the plethora of online fabric shops. There is plenty of cheaper fabric to be found, especially at national craft chain stores. Its weave is much looser than that of the high-quality fabric, and after several washes you may notice wear and pulls or pills. For quilts you plan to keep for a while, invest in the higher-quality fabric. I always use 100% cotton because it is natural, durable, and easy to manage, and it will shrink evenly. To avoid wonky shrinkage issues down the road, be sure to preshrink the fabric if you plan to machine wash your quilt.

Choose as many different colors/patterns as you like for the collage. I recommend choosing a variety of solids, textured solids, batiks, and monochromatic prints. By monochromatic print, I mean a print that is all or mostly one color. I avoid including more than one or two prints with negative (white) space because they tend to break up the collage.

Preparing materials

Background Fabric

For the collage background, I recommend a solid color or a very simple print that does not detract from the collage. If the collage will cover the entire quilt, a simple muslin fabric or interfacing would be perfect. For quilts with a pieced background, I usually choose solids, textured solids, or simple prints to allow the collage to stand out. For ideas, see Quick Pieced Backgrounds (page 30).

Backing Fabric

Typically this is one fabric that will cover the whole back of the quilt, but if you want to piece a few fabrics together for a more interesting back, go for it! The fabric can be whatever you like: a fun print, a solid color, or even a cotton flannel to make it nice and soft.

Binding Fabric

Binding is the finished edge of a quilt. Choose whatever fabric you like—I prefer 100% cotton. If you choose a print, consider that the binding will show only about ½″ wide around the quilt, so larger-scale prints will be cut off.

Batting

This is the middle, insulating layer of the quilt. Batting comes in a variety of types, available packaged or on a bolt. When choosing the batting, decide on the fiber and loft first.

FIBER

Batting can be made of cotton, polyester, cotton/polyester blend, or wool fibers, to name a few. What you choose is completely a matter of preference.

Polyester batting will not shrink and is usually less expensive than other types, but it is more difficult to machine quilt and has the tendency to beard. *Bearding* is the migration of the fibers though the layers of fabric; after this process starts, it can't be stopped. To reduce the risk of bearding, buy a high-quality polyester batting. Polyester batting tends to be slightly fuller, makes the quilting stand out a bit more than cotton batting, and is hypoallergenic.

Cotton batting will shrink when washed, giving the quilt a crinkled, vintage look. Cotton is easier than polyester to machine quilt because it grips the fabric, preventing a lot of slipping of the fabric layers. Unlike polyester, cotton does not have the tendency to beard.

Poly/cotton blends are usually made up of 80% cotton and 20% polyester. Poly/cotton is similar to the cotton option but usually less expensive, and it won't shrink as much when washed.

Wool batting has a lovely drape, defines stitches well, is easy to handle, and makes a very warm quilt. However, it is usually more expensive than the previous options and, like polyester, has the tendency to beard. Higher-quality wool batting may beard less.

LOFT

Next, choose high-loft (fluffy), medium-loft, or low-loft (thin) batting. Traditionally, quilts are made with low-loft batting, which allows you to quilt smoothly, without bunching or bulk. High-loft batting is great for a fluffy comforter that you plan to tie or quilt with lines further apart (see Quilting, page 42).

Also on the market is fusible batting. Fusible batting can be found in both polyester and cotton blends. It has a steam-activated adhesive in the fibers to allow for easy basting. Refer to Fusible Batting (page 41) for more information. You can find fusible batting at many major fabric stores or online.

I use low-loft cotton batting for my quilts. I don't mind the slight shrinkage, and I think it is so much easier to baste and quilt with cotton batting. I love Warm & Natural batting by The Warm Company.

Fusible Web

Fusible web is a heat-activated adhesive on a roll of nonstick paper. Place the fabric on the adhesive, press with an iron, and the adhesive is transferred to the fabric. After the adhesive is transferred, it is dry to the touch. You can then remove the paper, place the fabric on another fabric, and press with an iron to adhere. All the fabric in your collage will need fusible web. It is only 17″ wide, so I recommend buying twice as much as the yardage of the fabric for the collage. Of the various types available, I recommend Pellon's Heavy-Duty Wonder-Under for its extra-strong fusing that holds the pieces in place. You can buy it by the yard in most major craft/fabric stores or online.

NOTE If you want a more flexible collage, you can use lightweight fusible web, but be warned that some pieces could come loose after a lot of handling when you do the topstitching.

Thread

I use clear thread to topstitch my collage. You could use a color you like, but it will change the look of the collage. It can change the look for the better, but I typically choose clear thread because I want the fabrics I choose to stand out more than the stitches. If you do choose a clear thread (also called invisible or monofilament), go for a high-quality thread! It may cost a few dollars more, but it will save you a lot of headaches in the end. Cheap clear thread has the tendency to melt, break, get brittle after many washes, and cause a lot of tension issues with your machine. I recommend Superior Threads MonoPoly and Coats & Clark Transparent Polyester thread. I have had bad experiences with nylon thread, so I stick with polyester.

You may need to adjust the thread tension on your machine when using clear thread. I use white cotton thread in my bobbin when topstitching a collage. Clear thread in the bobbin can sometimes cause issues. I use a cotton thread to appliqué stitch around my collaged image (see *Tamed Fox*, page 51, as an example). My favorites are Aurifil 50-weight 100% cotton and Coats & Clark 100% cotton.

Interfacing

This is the foundation piece you build the collage on. I recommend using lightweight, *nonfusible* interfacing. I use Pellon lightweight, sew-in, non-woven interfacing.

Optional Fabrics

BORDER FABRIC

Borders aren't often used in modern quilting, but a border can be an excellent design element and easily add size to a quilt. If my quilt design is quite busy, I'll often add a solid border for a cleaner look. Adding a print or even a few different fabrics pieced together as a border can add a lot of interest as well. See Borders (page 37) for ideas and formulas to calculate yardage.

SLEEVE FABRIC

If you plan to hang your quilt on the wall, the easiest way to do so is by adding a fabric sleeve to the back of the quilt. It can be made from the same fabric as the backing or something totally different (see Hanging Sleeve, page 48).

Basic Sewing Supplies

See Resources (page 109) as needed.

A MARKING PENS

Use any of the various types of marking pens on the market, but be sure to test the pen on scrap fabric before using it on your quilt.

B ROTARY CUTTER

Rotary cutters come in many different brands and sizes. I love my Dritz, Omnigrid, and Olfa rotary cutters, rulers, and mats. A 45mm rotary cutter should be sufficient for most projects. I also regularly use an 18mm rotary cutter when cutting out precise and tight angles in my collages.

C ROTARY MAT

Choose a self-healing mat in whatever size is appropriate for your work space. The larger mats are easier to use, requiring less shifting and folding, but all will work just fine.

D RULER

Choose a quilting ruler that is as long as either the length or width of your cutting mat.

E STRAIGHT PINS

Use them to pin your cut-out collage to the background fabric.

F SAFETY PINS

If you plan to pin baste your quilt (see Basting, page 40), you will need plenty of safety pins. I place pins every 2″ when I baste. Dritz's curved basting pins are great for this purpose.

G BINDING CLIPS

Binding clips are not a necessity, but they make the binding process *much* easier. One package, any size, should be sufficient.

H FABRIC SCISSORS

You will need at least one pair of sharp fabric scissors for the projects and process in this book. I recommend a large pair (around 8″) and a small pair (around 4″–5″).

I IRON

Any iron with a steam setting will work. Higher-quality irons make the ironing process much quicker. I love my Oliso Smart Iron.

J SEAM SEALANT

I use Fray Check on the raw edges of the collages for bed or lap quilts to prevent fraying over time. Of all the different types of fray gels on the market, Dritz Fray Check is the only brand I have used that works really well without getting gunky or discoloring the fabric. Be sure to test the gel on scrap fabric before using it on your quilt.

Prewashing Fabric

Opinions differ on whether or not it is necessary to prewash fabric. If you get colorfast fabrics that all have the same fiber content and you don't mind the risk of uneven shrinkage, you can probably skip this step. If you are using different fiber blends, or if you aren't sure whether or not a fabric is colorfast, you should prewash. Here is how:

1. Throw the fabric in the washer (if it can be machine washed—if not, hand wash). Use a couple of dye-absorbing sheets (I use Shout Color Catcher sheets) to prevent dye from bleeding from one fabric onto another. If you do not use a dye absorber, wash similar colors together. If your quilt will have a white front and a red back (for example), wash the fabrics separately!

2. Tumble dry (without fabric softener) and iron (without starch).

> **NOTE** If your fabric is hand dyed, or if you are unsure whether it is colorfast, do the following:
>
> 1. Hand wash the fabrics in warm water one at a time.
>
> 2. If after a few washes a fabric is still bleeding dye, submerge it in white vinegar to set the dye, and rinse it thoroughly. Alternatively, use Retayne, a product designed to stop fabric bleeding.
>
> 3. Rewash, tumble dry, and then iron.
>
> If the fabric continues to bleed after the treatment, do not use it in your quilt. Very few fabrics need this level of attention.

Preparing the collage fabric

Sizes and Shapes

When deciding how to cut your fabric, consider two things: the size and the shape of the pieces.

Size

Large and small collaged pieces create very different looks. If you are trying to show-case a particular fabric, you may decide upon larger pieces. If you are going for a mosaic, pointillist, or expressionist look, smaller pieces would better suit the style. The size of your quilt and image will, of course, factor in also. Larger quilts and images may warrant larger collage pieces, while mini quilts may call for smaller pieces. Consider, though, that the smaller the pieces, the more densely you will need to topstitch or quilt later. A happy medium of pieces about 3″–4″ wide and long is usually good. Before choosing, read Creating the Collage (page 26) and choose a method to topstitch and quilt your collage.

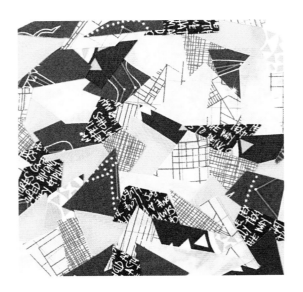

Different-sized pieces can create very different looks.

Shape

Different collage shapes all create different looks: squares, rectangles, strips, triangles, circles, rounded strips, wild/random shapes, and more. Think about the design of the collage. What shape(s) would represent or complement the design best? For example, long vertical strips are good to represent the wood grain of trees, small circles in different white fabrics are perfect for the wool on a lamb, and rounded strips can create movement in a collage of the sun.

My two favorite collage patterns are wood grain (strips) and mosaic (wild, random pieces). The following are some different possibilities.

Squares

Strips

Triangles

Swirls

This wood grain collage pattern is one of my favorites.

Circles

Random mosaic

SCRAPS AND SPRAY ADHESIVE I always start with large pieces of fabric and apply fusible web to the back before cutting them into smaller pieces. If you would like to start with smaller pieces, such as scraps from other projects, you might find it easier to use your favorite spray-on fusible web rather than cutting and fusing numerous small pieces of fusible web. When using a spray fusible, always work in a well-ventilated area, away from open flames.

Applying Fusible Web

Use fusible web on all the collage fabrics. It's easiest to apply fusible web to fabrics *before* you cut them.

1. Follow the manufacturer's instructions to apply the fusible web to the *back* of the fabrics you will be using on your collage.

2. Remove the paper from the back of the fabrics *before* you cut.

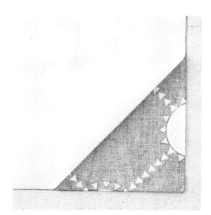

Cutting the Fabric

Do not worry about being precise! You will collage these pieces, and no one will be able to tell if an angle is exactly correct. You don't need to use a ruler—just make quick cuts with your rotary cutter. I like the wild, imperfect look that method creates. Still, if you are going for a more geometric or precise aesthetic, by all means, measure away.

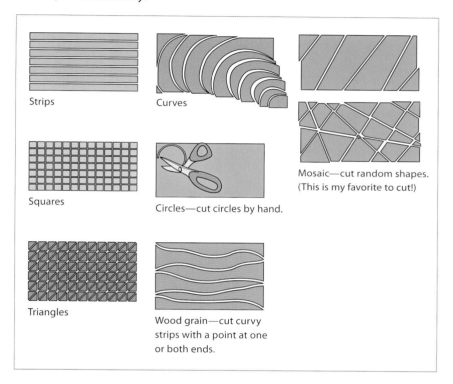

Strips

Curves

Squares

Circles—cut circles by hand.

Mosaic—cut random shapes. (This is my favorite to cut!)

Triangles

Wood grain—cut curvy strips with a point at one or both ends.

Cutting Tips

1. *Use a hard surface.*

2. *If cutting a lot of pieces, fold or layer your fabric to cut two, three, or four times as many pieces at once!*

3. *To provide the best leverage, stand over your cutting surface.*

4. *Cut away from yourself!*

5. *Place cut pieces into stacks to keep them organized.*

Creating the collage

Getting Started

Prepare the Space

Find a large surface on which it is safe to iron; a craft table is ideal. If you are using a table with a finish, be sure to cover it adequately: It will be exposed to heat and steam from the iron, and the adhesive from the fusible web can go through the foundation fabric and leave a residue on the table. A big towel works well.

Try putting all of your cut collage pieces in stacks on a tray. This makes it easy to move them around while you collage. If you are using a pattern, have it ready and make sure you can see it through the fabric on which you will collage. If you can't see it, cut out the design and use it as a stencil instead.

Choose Your Approach

Note: Read this entire section before you proceed.

There are two ways to create a collage: collaging directly on the background fabric, or collaging on scrap fabric or interfacing and then sewing the collage to the background. Depending on the design, you may need to do one or the other.

APPROACH 1: COLLAGING DIRECTLY ON THE BACKGROUND FABRIC

With this method, you create the collage, press it, and sew it directly to the background fabric. The nice thing about this method is you can skip the step of securing your collage to the background fabric, making it ideal for designs that are too complex to cut out. I use this method with my trees when they have a lot of tangled roots and branches. These elements would take forever to cut out and be difficult to attach to the background smoothly. This method does, however, makes collaging a particular shape more difficult, since you have to make sure the fabric you arrange is forming the shape desired. Do not use this method if your design is very complex and requires precise shapes, as with *Around the World* (page 71). This technique also makes topstitching the collage much more cumbersome because of the added bulk of the background fabric to maneuver through your sewing machine.

APPROACH 2: CREATING THE COLLAGE SEPARATELY

With this method, start with a plain, inexpensive piece of material. I recommend a lightweight, nonfusible interfacing because it is low in cost and won't fray when you cut the shape out. I recommend this technique if your design is complex and requires precise shapes. This technique also makes topstitching a lot easier, especially if the collage is significantly smaller than the background fabric, as with *Tamed Fox* (page 51) or *Blocks for Elephants* (page 61). If your collage is large and has elements that would be difficult to smoothly attach to the background fabric, consider using the method described in Collaging Directly on the Background Fabric (below).

Collaging

Collaging Directly on the Background Fabric

Note: If you are using a pieced background (see Quick Pieced Backgrounds, page 30), you will need to make it before you begin collaging.

1. If you are using a pattern, tape it to the table. If you cannot see the pattern through the background fabric, cut out the pattern to use as a stencil.

2. Trace or draw the design on the background fabric using chalk or another marking utensil that will not leave permanent marks. Remove the pattern and set it aside. If you are brave and plan to collage without first sketching the design, skip these 2 steps.

3. Decide whether you want certain sections layered on top (often more detailed sections are handled this way). Begin with the sections that will be on the bottom. If you are not concerned with having certain sections layered above others, simply choose a corner to start in.

4. Using the lines you drew as a guide, begin placing fabric pieces on the background fabric. Overlap the fabrics; you do not want to see the background through your collage at all after you are finished. Be sure to stay within the lines, and be conscious of the overall shape you are creating. **B**

5. After you have finished a section, use an iron to press and adhere that part of your collage.

PRESS, DON'T IRON! Note that there is a difference between ironing and pressing! Ironing (sliding the iron back and forth over the fabric) stretches fabric and will shift the pieces in your collage.

To press, place the iron directly on the collage for 6–10 seconds (follow the fusible web manufacturer's instructions for how long and for the proper iron temperature), and then lift straight up. Continue this pressing and lifting pattern until the section is adhered.

6. Continue collaging a section at a time, pressing after the completion of each section, until you have finished your collage. **C**

A Trace pattern onto background fabric.

B Collage fabric.

C Collage and press until finished.

Creating the Collage Separately

There are only a few differences between this process and the one described in Collaging Directly on the Background Fabric (page 27).

1. Draw or trace the design onto lightweight interfacing using chalk or pencil. Go over the tracing with a dark piece of chalk or marker when you are satisfied with the shape. You want the lines to be dark enough that you can see them from the back when you cut the shape out, but not so dark that you can see them through the collaged fabric on the front. **A**

> **NOTE** If you use a marking pen that bleeds when steamed, be sure to trace the pattern onto the back side of the interfacing to avoid having the marker bleed onto the fabric. If you do this, you must draw or print the pattern in reverse.

2. Collage the fabric as in the previous section, and press. **B**

3. Use the lines you can see through the back of the interfacing to cut out the design. **C**

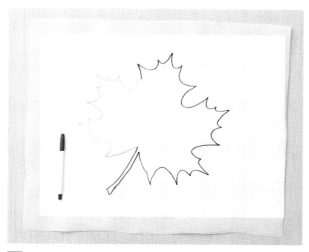
A Trace pattern onto interfacing.

B Collage and press.

C Cut out design.

Quick Pieced *backgrounds*

Collages look great on solid backgrounds, but juxtaposing a collaged design with a pieced background is fun and can add a lot of interest. Here are some quick and simple options for a pieced background (they make great stand-alone quilts too!). These are perfect choices for a first-time quilter or someone who would like to whip together a pieced background in a few hours.

Pellon produces a wonderful product called Quilter's Grid and Quilter's Grid On-Point (see Resources, page 109). Quilter's Grid is a light-weight, nonwoven, fusible material with a grid printed on it, which makes piecing patchwork a breeze! Quilter's Grid On-Point is exactly the same, except that the grid is printed at a 45° angle, so the squares are on the diagonal. Each creates a different look, but they are used in the same way.

Quick Squares

The Quilter's Grid and Quilter's Grid On-Point have a grid with 1″ squares. This method may be done using any size square. Fabric squares as small as 1″ look great, but they take a lot longer to piece than larger squares. Using 4″–8″ fabric squares goes much faster. Place the fabric squares on the Quilter's Grid, fuse them in place, and then sew them together following the grid lines for perfectly pieced rows of squares.

If possible, cut the squares in multiples of 1″ so they will fit in the grid. However, if you need the finished squares to be a multiple of 1″, then the cut square cut size will be ½″ larger. The squares should still be placed right next to each other so that you can use the grid lines as a guide to keep them straight.

To determine how large to cut the Quilter's Grid, first determine the size of the cut squares (by adding ½″ to the finished square size for seams) and how many squares wide and tall the quilt will be. To calculate the width, multiply the cut square size by the number of squares across the quilt. For the length, multiply the cut square size by the number of squares down the quilt. This is the size to cut the Quilter's Grid.

For example, for a quilt with 5″ finished squares that will be 10 squares wide and 12 squares long, cut the Quilter's Grid 55″ × 66″:

$$(5″ + ½″) \times 10 = 55″$$

$$(5″ + ½″) \times 12 = 66″$$

Cut and piece the Quilter's Grid to 55″ × 66″. Once all the seams are sewn, the quilt top will be 50″ × 60″.

To determine what size to cut the Quilter's Grid On-Point, decide what size the cut squares will be and how many squares wide and tall the quilt will be. Calculate the cut square size by adding ½″ for seams. Multiply the cut square size by 1.414 to get the diagonal measurement of the square. To calculate the width of the grid, multiply this diagonal measurement by the number of squares across the quilt. For the length, multiply the diagonal measurement by the number of squares down the quilt. This is the size to cut the Quilter's Grid On-Point.

For example, for a quilt with 5″ finished squares that will be 5 squares wide and 6 squares long, cut the Quilter's Grid On-Point 39″ × 47″:

$$[(5″ + ½″) \times 1.414] \times 5 = 38.885; \text{ round up to } 39″$$

$$[(5″ + ½″) \times 1.414] \times 6 = 46.662; \text{ round up to } 47″$$

Cut and piece the Quilter's Grid On-Point to 39″ × 47″. Once all the seams are sewn, the quilt top will be 35¾″ × 43″.

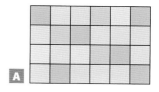

1. Cut the Quilter's Grid or Quilter's Grid On-Point and piece together to the needed size. To piece the Quilter's Grid, place the nonfusible sides together and sew a ¼″ seam along the printed line. Finger-press the seam open. Since the Quilter's Grid is fusible, do not press the seam with an iron! Alternately, if you have a Teflon pressing cloth, you can overlap the seams and fuse the pieces together just along the seamline if you prefer.

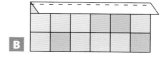

2. Cut the fabric squares to the needed size.

3. Place the squares on the Quilter's Grid either in a pattern or in random order. Use the gridlines to help keep them lined up. Place them right next to each other, not overlapping or leaving a big gap. (If you overlap or gap slightly, that is okay, as long as it is less than ¼″.) **A**

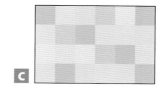

4. Carefully press the pieces in place, according to the manufacturer's instructions.

5. Fold the first row over, with right sides facing each other. Sew together with a ¼″ seam down the row. Repeat for the rest of the horizontal rows. **B**

6. Flip the quilt top over and press all the seams in the same direction. If the seams are bulky, trim them (just don't cut the thread!).

7. Repeat Steps 5 and 6 for all the vertical rows. **C**

Half-Square Triangle Background

Half-square triangles offer so many design possibilities! Following is a lovely shortcut to make them.

1. Determine the desired size of the finished quilt and size of the blocks, as in the previous section. Calculate the size of the Quilter's Grid needed.

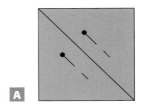

A

2. Cut the squares 1″ larger than their planned finished size. Example: For 5″ finished squares, cut squares 6″ × 6″.

3. Place right sides of the squares together. Use a ruler to trace a line diagonally across the top square in chalk or another marking utensil. Pin together. Repeat for all of the squares. **A**

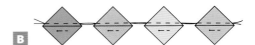

B

4. Sew the first seam ¼″ away from this centerline. Do not break or cut the thread. When you finish this set, simply lift the presser foot and pull the sewn squares out about an inch behind the machine. Place the next set under the foot and sew a ¼″ seam down the same side of the line. Repeat for all of the sets until you have a long chain of squares. Break the thread at the end of the chain. **B**

C

5. Flip the chain around and sew a ¼″ seam down the other side of the line. Do the same for the rest of the chain. **C**

6. Cut the sets apart.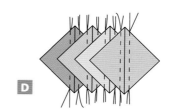

7. Using a ruler and rotary cutter, cut along the chalk line on each set.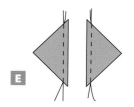

8. Press the seam open. **F**

9. Using the rotary cutter and ruler, trim the squares to the finished size. **G**

10. Follow Quick Squares, Steps 3–7 (page 31) to finish the quilt top. **H**

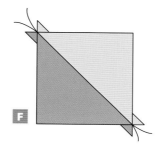

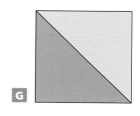

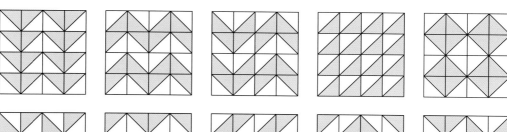

H Possible combinations of half-square triangles for backgrounds

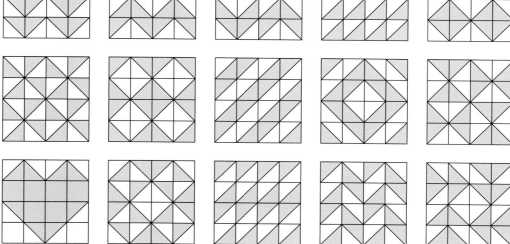

Stitching the Collage to the quilt top

Tip If you create your collage separately, you can topstitch before or after you cut out the shape. It depends on the complexity of the shape. If the shape is really simple (such as the one in Blocks for Elephants, *page 61*), without any long thin strands that are hard to topstitch alone (the needle tends to push thin strands into the machine), you can topstitch after cutting. If the design is complex (like a tree with lots of branches, or leaves with thin stems), it's best to topstitch before cutting out the shape.

Topstitching Method

NOTE If you plan to quilt tightly (1/8″–1/2″, depending on the size of the pieces), you can skip this step.

The purpose of this step is to permanently secure all of the collage pieces. You are only sewing through your collage right now; in Finishing the Quilt (page 37), you will quilt together the backing, batting, and quilt top. If you plan to display the quilt rather than use it, you might prefer to use the method described in Tulle Overlay Method (page 36) as an alternative to topstitching.

1. Thread your machine with clear polyester thread (refer to Thread, page 19).

2. Whenever you sew, always lock the stitches. This means that at the beginning and end of any stitching, you reverse a few stitches to secure the thread in place. Simply sew a couple of stitches forward and then reverse over those stitches.

3. The goal is to secure all of the sides and corners of each piece. You can do this by sewing straight lines 1/8″–1/4″ apart; or sew around all the raw edges (this is easiest to do in free-motion mode—if you aren't sure how to set your machine up this way, refer to the free-motion quilting settings in your machine's manual). You may also stitch several inches forward and then backward, in a zigzag pattern all over the collage. Since the thread is clear, you do not need to worry about making a precise pattern; just be sure to sew over all the corners! You can also sew along

the contours of the image to help it stand out. I find that as long as my stitching is distributed evenly over the collage, it looks great in the end. The more wear the quilt will get, the more densely you want to sew the collage to prevent fraying. For the photos, I used a contrasting thread so that you can see the stitches; however, this stitching should be made with clear polyester thread.

4. For quilts that will get a lot of use, use a seam sealant gel along all the raw edges at this stage to ensure they will not fray even after many machine washings. Seam sealants can be found at most major fabric stores (see Materials and Supplies, page 16).

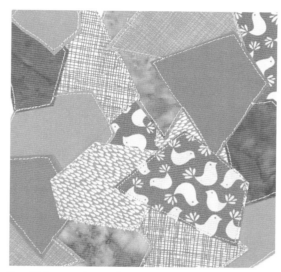

Topstitch around raw edges.

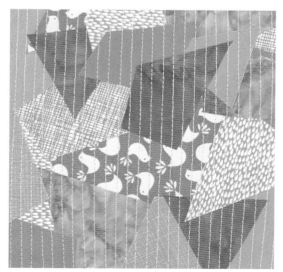

Topstitch in straight lines.

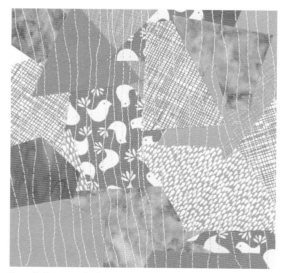

Topstitch in wonky lines.

Tulle Overlay Method

This is an alternative for those of you who prefer to sew less. The tulle is virtually invisible, but it holds all of the pieces in place. With a tulle overlay you don't need to do all the topstitching (page 34). This is a nice option for wallhangings when you have collaged a large area. I would not recommend this option for quilts that will get a lot of wear, since the tulle could tear after much use. Be sure that you begin this step with enough time to baste and quilt the project in the same day, because the adhesive spray will dissipate after a day or two. Choose a color of tulle that blends in with the majority of the fabric. I recommend taking the finished quilt top (or fabric you plan to use) to the store with you and placing different colors of tulle on top to see which blends in best.

You'll need the finished quilt top, tulle, and temporary adhesive spray.

1. Cut the piece of tulle about 4″ longer and wider than the quilt top.

2. Using temporary adhesive spray, spray the collage, and then promptly place the tulle onto the quilt top. The spray should not harm the fabric, but test it on a sample area / scrap fabric first.

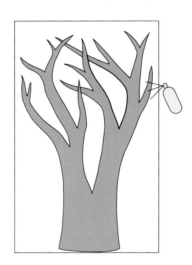

3. Smooth out the wrinkles.

4. Immediately baste and quilt (refer to Finishing the Quilt, page 37).

NOTE Be sure not to press the iron directly on the tulle—it will melt. To press, flip it over and press the back of the quilt. You may also steam either the front or the back, being careful not to touch the tulle with the iron.

Finishing *the quilt*

Borders

Borders are optional, but they can add interest, balance, and size. For a quilt that needs another design element to spice it up, add a pieced border or a border with a contrasting color or striking pattern. For quilts that are slightly busy, add a solid-color border to balance the more intricate design. Finally, borders are an easy way to enlarge a quilt top. There are no rules as to the number of borders in a quilt—add one, two, or six borders if you feel so inclined! The types of borders you can add are mitered, unmitered, and what I call "fast borders."

Mitered Borders

1. Decide on the border width. Measure the length of the quilt top and cut 2 border strips this length plus about 2½ times the border width. Repeat for the width of the quilt top.

2. Attach the first border strip to the quilt top, right sides together. Sew a ¼˝ seam allowance, and stop ¼˝ from either end. **A**

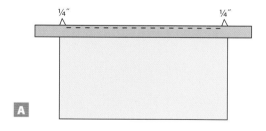

3. Move the first border out of the way and attach the second border, also starting and stopping ¼˝ from either end. Repeat for the 2 remaining borders. **B**

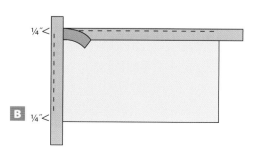

4. At each corner, fold the quilt in half along the diagonal, creating a 45° line with the border. Using a ruler, mark the 45° angle on the border, starting where the stitches left off.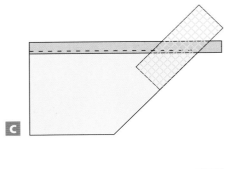

5. Sew along that marked line.

6. Check to see that the border lies flat, and then trim the excess fabric ¼˝ from the seam. Press the seam open. Repeat for the other corners.

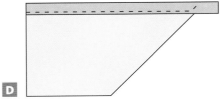

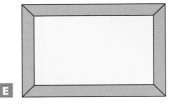

Unmitered Borders

1. Measure the width of the quilt top, and cut 2 border strips equal to this measurement.

2. Attach the top and bottom borders by sewing them, right sides together, to the quilt top with a ¼˝ seam allowance. Press seams open.

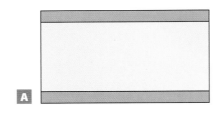

3. Measure the length of the quilt top with the top and bottom borders attached, and cut the side borders equal to this measurement. Be sure you have measured the full length of the quilt top with the *top and bottom borders included!* The most common mistake people make when adding borders is not making the second pair long enough to include the length added by the first pair.

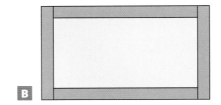

4. Attach the right and left borders to the quilt top with a ¼˝ seam. Press seams open.

Fast Borders

This is the method I use most often because I am not super concerned with precision.

1. Find the perimeter of the quilt top (remember: perimeter = side + side + side + side). Add the width of the border × 4. Then add about 10″ for good measure. So the formula is this:

   (side + side + side + side) + (border width × 4) + 10″

This is the length of border to cut.

2. Cut the border strips and then sew them into a long strip.

3. Pick a corner to start in. Place the border and quilt top right sides together, and sew with a ¼″ seam allowance.

4. When you get to the end of that side, cut the strip off at a 90° angle, even with the next side. Press the seam open. **A**

5. Attach the next border to the next side, lining it up with the border on the previous side. **B**

6. Repeat for the remaining sides. **C**

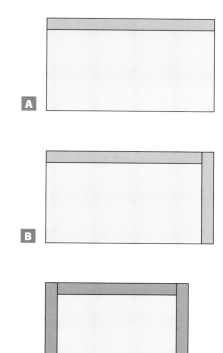

Basting

Basting holds together the three layers of the quilt (backing, batting, and quilt top) so they stay in place during the quilting process. There are three ways to easily baste: with safety pins, with fusible batting, and with basting spray.

Safety Pin Basting

This is the method I prefer, especially for larger quilts (larger than crib size). I don't like adding unnecessary chemicals (adhesives) to a quilt, and this method allows me to quilt more smoothly than the other two. For smooth quilting, be sure the layers are as flat and wrinkle free as possible.

1. Spread the backing on the floor, *right side down*, and tape the corners (and sides, if necessary) with pieces of masking tape.

2. Place the batting on top of the backing, and smooth out all wrinkles while not stretching the fibers too much. Tape in place, if needed.

3. Spread the quilt top on top of the batting, *right side up*. Smooth out all wrinkles, and tape in place, if needed. **A**

4. Begin placing the safety pins in the center, working out in a spiral pattern, placing them about 2″ apart. As you place them, smooth the layers, ensuring there are no wrinkles. This step can be tedious, but it is very important for a neatly finished quilt. **B**

When finished, remove the tape and get ready to quilt!

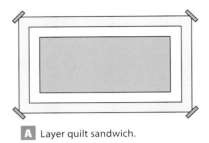

A Layer quilt sandwich.

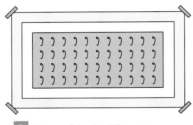

B Place safety pins 2″ apart.

Fusible Batting

Fusible batting and fusible fleece are available in a few different types. As with any batting, be sure to choose a high-quality product to avoid problems down the road (see Batting, page 18). Fusible batting has a heat-activated adhesive in the fibers. Layer the quilt top, fusible batting, and backing, and then press the quilt sandwich with steam. I often use fusible batting for smaller quilts.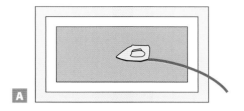

- -

Basting Spray

The layers in the quilt sandwich can be held together with basting spray. Due to the fumes, always use outdoors or in a well-ventilated area, and away from open flames.

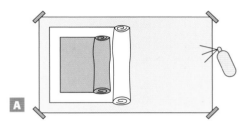

1. Layer the quilt sandwich; then roll the quilt top, and then the batting, back halfway. A

2. Spray the backing with the basting spray and then quickly unroll the batting and smooth out. B

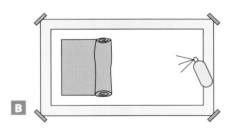

3. Next, spray the batting with the basting spray and then unroll and smooth out the quilt top. Be sure to smooth out all wrinkles—most basting sprays allow you to reposition the layers once or twice. Repeat for the other half.

I use basting spray only occasionally and, again, just for smaller projects, simply because it needs to be used in a well-ventilated area, which isn't always possible for me. In addition, excess spray can land beyond the quilt, leaving a sticky finish on the neighboring furniture and floor. It is also not the most eco-friendly option.

Quilting

Quilting simply means permanently attaching the three layers of the quilt together with thread. There are endless possibilities for how to quilt a quilt. Here are a few of my favorite patterns.

Wavy Line Pattern

This is my favorite beginner quilting pattern. It is very quick and hard to mess up! The lines are wavy, so imperfection is perfectly fine. Check your batting to see how wide you can quilt. I recommend setting the quilted waves 4″ or less apart.

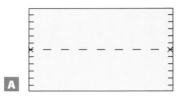

1. Using a piece of chalk or other erasable marking utensil, make a mark every 4″ (or however wide you choose to make the lines) on the top and bottom edges of your quilt. Be sure the marks on the top and bottom of the quilt line up with each other.

2. Find the mark in the middle of the quilt (I make these marks X's to easily identify them), and mark down the center of the quilt every 4″ or so to the bottom middle mark. This will be the guide for the first quilting column. **A**

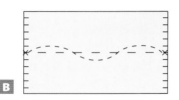

3. Using a darning or walking foot, start at the top middle mark (roll the side of the quilt that is under the sewing machine's arm inward to remove bulk), lock the stitches, and start stitching a wavy line down the center of the quilt, following the guide marks you made. After you get to the bottom middle mark, lock the stitches and cut the thread to end that column. This column will be a guide for the rest of the quilt, so be sure it goes relatively straight down the center of the quilt. **B**

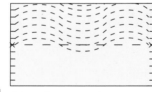

Echo column to end.

4. Use the first column you made as a guide for the rest of the columns. Start back at the top on the mark to the right of the center column, and make the second row, following the same wavy pattern as the first column. Repeat this process until you finish the rows on the right half. Flip the quilt around to complete the remaining rows, starting from the center and working your way out. **C D**

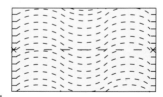

Flip around, and repeat for other side.

Stitch in-the-Ditch

Stitching in-the-ditch simply means stitching in the seams you created by piecing. It is a nice option if the background is pieced and you'd like to emphasize the pieces.

Straight-Line Quilting

Straight-line quilting is exactly what it sounds like, quilting in straight lines down or across the quilt. It is actually much trickier than it sounds, because one wonky line could be quite noticeable. I have done some straight-line quilting where I have intentionally made the lines a little wobbly, which turned out quite nice. Straight-line quilting is done just like the wavy line pattern except that the lines are, of course, straight rather than wavy.

Free-Motion Quilting

I do all of my quilting (except straight-line quilting) using free-motion quilting. In free-motion quilting, the machine is not feeding the quilt sandwich through; rather, the quilter is moving the quilt sandwich around under the needle to create the desired pattern. Most machine manuals have instructions for free-motion quilting settings. My machine instructs me to lower the feed dogs, but I have found that reducing the stitch length to zero accomplishes the same goal of keeping the feed dogs from moving the fabric, while avoiding a lot of thread issues. You may have to play with the settings a bit when you are first starting free-motion quilting to find what works best for your machine. I highly recommend the book *Free-Motion Quilting with Angela Walters* for more detail and instruction on this technique, along with dozens of beautiful patterns.

Binding

The binding is the finished edge of the quilt. Binding is one long strip of fabric folded in half, so one edge of the binding is raw and the other edge is folded. Using a sewing machine, sew the raw edge of the binding to the front of the quilt; then fold the binding around to the back of the quilt, and either hand or machine stitch the folded edge to the back of the quilt.

Hand stitching the folded edge to the back of the quilt is the traditional method. It is also the most neat and precise method. It does, however, take a while, so consider this when deciding whether to hand or machine stitch. I like to hand stitch the binding while sitting on the couch with a movie on, so I don't mind its taking a while. If you choose to hand stitch the back of the binding, cut the binding strips 2½˝ wide.

Machine finishing the binding is much quicker but does not look quite as neat (unless you are very talented). This option may be perfect for those of you who are not concerned with perfection and just want to finish the quilt. If you machine stitch the binding, cut the binding strips 3˝ wide, so the sewing machine is sure to catch the edge.

1. Cut binding fabric into 2½˝ strips (3˝ if machine finishing).

2. Connect all the strips into a long strip. To connect 2 strips, place 2 ends at right angles, right sides together, and sew a diagonal seam across the corner. Trim seam to ¼˝ and press open. Repeat until all strips are joined. **A**

3. At an end of the binding, fold a 45° angle and press. Trim the excess ¼˝ beyond the fold. Fold the whole piece of binding in half widthwise and press. **B C**

4. Place the binding (the end with the 45° angle) along the edge of the *front* of the quilt so the raw edges of the binding are lined up with the raw edges of the quilt sandwich. Make sure the 45° angle is several inches from the corner; I usually start my binding in the middle of the right-hand side of the quilt.

5. Using a walking foot, start sewing a few inches below the 45° angle, ⅜˝ from the raw edge. Sew until you are ⅜˝ from the first corner, backstitch, cut the thread, and remove the quilt from the machine. **D**

6. Fold the binding up, creating a 45° angle at the corner. Finger-press that angle. **E**

7. Fold the binding down over that 45° angle, with the fold even with the raw edge of the quilt, and the raw edge of the binding even with the next side of the quilt. The corner should be nice and squared. **F**

8. Place the needle ⅜˝ from each edge of the corner and continue sewing. **G**

9. Repeat Steps 5–8 for each corner.

10. Continue sewing until you are 1˝ from the beginning of the binding. Backstitch, cut thread, and remove the quilt from the machine.

11. Trim the binding so it is about 1˝–2˝ longer than the triangular opening. Tuck the loose binding into the triangular opening. **H**

12. Continue sewing the remainder of the binding until you reach the first stitches. Backstitch and cut the thread. **I**

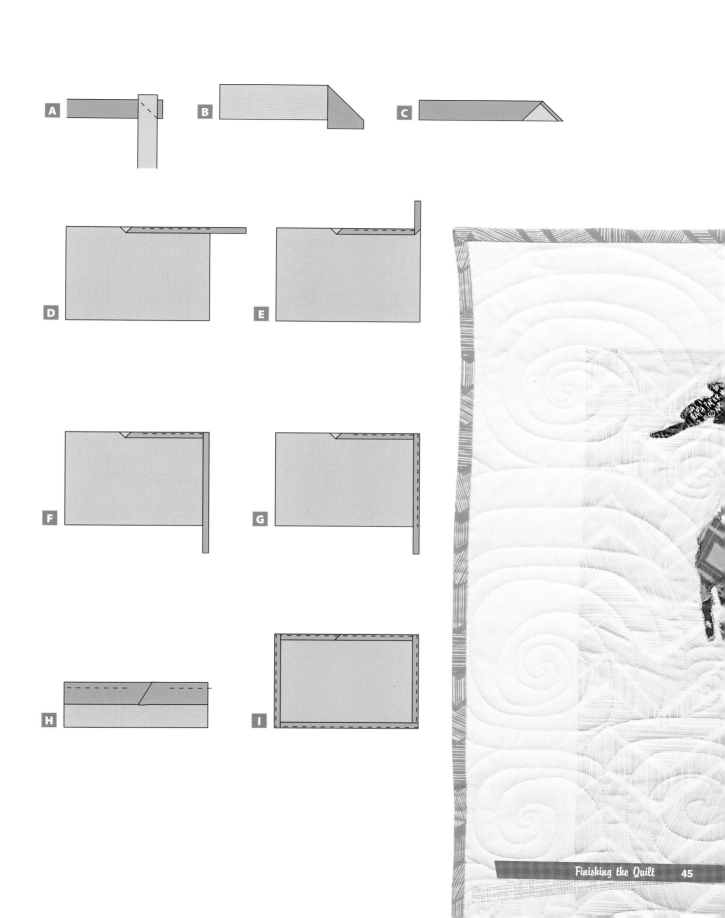

Hand Finishing

If you are hand finishing the binding, pull out your sewing needle, thimble, and some thread. Find a comfy spot to settle in for a lot of stitches.

1. Fold the binding over; it should extend about ⅛″ over the stitches you just made. Place binding clips every inch or so to secure the binding while you stitch.

2. Thread the needle and tie a knot at the end of the thread (I cut my thread about a yard long, but you may prefer a shorter length). Make a first stitch tucked up under the binding to hide the knot. Begin stitching the very edge of the binding, picking up a few threads of the backing. Be sure to sew just into the backing, not all 3 layers. You do not want the stitches to show on the front of the quilt. **A**

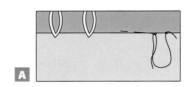

3. Continue until you reach the corner. **B**

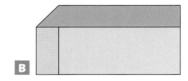

4. Fold the binding on the back side over to create a nice mitered corner like the front. **C**

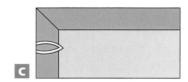

5. Continue stitching around the corner. Continue until finished.

Machine Finishing

1. Fold the binding over; it should extend about ¼″ over the stitches you just made. Place binding clips every inch or so to secure the binding while you stitch.

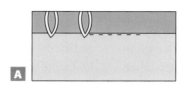

2. Fold a nice miter on the back at the corners. Pin carefully.

3. With the quilt top facing up, begin stitching in-the-ditch along the edge of the binding (not *on* the binding). Use thread that blends with the quilt top. The stitches should be so close to the binding that they are barely visible. **A**

4. At the corners, continue sewing (slowly!) until you reach a single stitch over the lovely fold you just made. Reverse a stitch. Put the needle down, lift the presser foot, and pivot the quilt 90°. Lower the presser foot, backstitch a stitch, and continue sewing along the edge. Repeat until you've sewn all of the binding! **B**

Hanging Sleeve

A hanging sleeve can be added to the top of the back of the quilt for a hanging rod to slip into so that it can be displayed on a wall or in a show. Most shows recommend a 4″ finished sleeve, which means you will start with a piece of fabric 9″ wide.

1. Cut a strip 9″ wide by the width of the quilt.

2. Fold the sleeve in half along the length and sew together with a ¼″ seam. There is no need to turn the sleeve tube "right side out" because this seam will be placed toward the back of the quilt.

3. Hem each of the narrow ends of the tube by turning under ¼″ twice and stitching the hem. This insures that the sleeve will now be 1″ shorter than the width of the quilt and will not show.

4. Press the sleeve with the long seam down the center of a side.

5. Pin a long edge of the sleeve to the back of the quilt, about 1″ below the top edge and ½″ from each side, with the long seam against the back of the quilt.

6. Pin the lower edge to the quilt, keeping the back, seamed side flat against the quilt and shifting the pressed edge about ½″ up toward the top fold. This creates a gap in the sleeve that will allow for the dimension of the hanging rod.

7. Hand stitch both long edges and the back edge of the sleeve at each end to the quilt back, being careful not to stitch through to the front of the quilt.

THE PROJECTS

Tamed Fox

size shown: 56½″ × 68½″ (lap size)

I originally made *Tamed Fox* for a good friend who was having her first baby. It was made of pumpkin-, olive-, and chocolate-colored fabrics (terrible flavor combination, but lovely color combination) and was a big hit at the baby shower. I've since made it many more times in a variety of colors and sizes. One of my favorite books is *The Little Prince* by Antoine de Saint-Exupéry, and the sweet fox that teaches the Little Prince about love and friendship was the inspiration for this design. The fox would also look great on its own, if you don't want to include the border!

MATERIALS	Baby/wall 42½″ × 51½″	Lap 56½″ × 68½″	Twin 70½″ × 85½″	Full/queen* 84½″ × 96½″	King** 112½″ × 105½″
Background	1 yard	1⅝ yards	3 yards	3½ yards	4⅞ yards
Various orange fabrics	½ yard total (if reducing fox)	¾ yard total	1 yard total	1¼ yards total	1½ yards total
Orange accent fabric	½ yard	½ yard	½ yard	1 yard	1 yard
White	1 yard	1⅛ yards	1¾ yards	2⅜ yards	2¾ yards
Black	1 yard	1⅛ yards	1¾ yards	2⅜ yards	2¾ yards
Backing	2⅞ yards	3⅝ yards	5¼ yards	7¾ yards	9½ yards
Batting	50″ × 59″	64″ × 76″	78″ × 93″	92″ × 104″	120″ × 113″
Binding	½ yard	⅝ yard	¾ yard	⅞ yard	1 yard
Lightweight, nonfusible interfacing	16″ × 23″ (if reducing)	20″ × 30″	28″ × 42″	32″ × 49″	36″ × 55″
Paper-backed fusible web	2 yards	2½ yards	3 yards	4½ yards	5 yards
Fox pattern (on pullout page P1)	As is for a large fox, or reduce 75%.	As is	Enlarge 150%.	Enlarge 175%.	Enlarge 200%.

* Full/queen-size quilt has 1 less row in the vertical borders.

** King-size quilt has 2 more rows in the horizontal borders and 2 fewer rows in the vertical borders.

Additional supplies

- **Thread:** clear polyester, orange, black, white

CUTTING

WOF = width of fabric

	Baby/wall	Lap	Twin	Full/queen	King*
Background	30½″ × 39½″	40½″ × 52½″	Cut 2 panels 50½″ × WOF and piece along the 50½″ sides. Cut to 50½″ × 65½″.	Cut 2 panels 60½″ × WOF and piece along the 60½″ sides. Cut to 60½″ × 72½″.	Cut 2 panels 84½″ × WOF and piece along the 84½″ sides. Cut to 84½″ × 77½″.
White	Cut 54 squares 4″ × 4″.	Cut 54 squares 5″ × 5″.	Cut 54 squares 6″ × 6″.	Cut 52 squares 7″ × 7″.	Cut 54 squares 8″ × 8″.
Black	Cut 54 squares 4″ × 4″.	Cut 54 squares 5″ × 5″.	Cut 54 squares 6″ × 6″.	Cut 52 squares 7″ × 7″.	Cut 54 squares 8″ × 8″.
Backing	Cut 2 panels 50″ × WOF and piece along the 50″ sides. Cut to 50″ × 59″.	Cut 2 panels 64″ × WOF and piece along the 64″ sides. Cut to 64″ × 76″.	Cut 2 panels 93″ × WOF and piece along the 93″ sides. Cut to 78″ × 93″.	Cut 3 panels 92″ × WOF and piece along the 92″ sides. Cut to 92″ × 104″.	Cut 3 panels 113″ × WOF and piece along the 113″ sides. Cut to 120″ × 113″.
Binding (page 44)	Cut 6 strips 2½″ × WOF.	Cut 7 strips 2½″ × WOF.	Cut 9 strips 2½″ × WOF.	Cut 10 strips 2½″ × WOF.	Cut 12 strips 2½″ × WOF.

* Since the king-size quilt is wider than it is long, be sure to arrange the background accordingly before sewing on the fox.

Border

	Baby/wall	Lap	Twin	Full/queen	King
Finished block size	3″	4″	5″	6″	7″
Geese blocks	46	46	46	44	46
Corner blocks	4	4	4	4	4
Blocks in horizontal borders	10	10	10	10	12
Blocks in vertical borders	13	13	13	12	11

Prepare the Collage Fabric

Refer to Preparing the Collage Fabric (page 22).

1. Apply fusible web to the back of the orange collage and accent fabric (see Applying Fusible Web, page 25).

2. After the web is applied, remove the paper and cut the orange fabric using the random mosaic technique in Cutting the Fabric (page 25). *Do not cut the accent fabric.*

3. Apply fusible web to a scrap of black fabric for the eyes and nose.

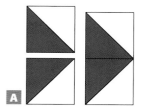

Make the Border

All seam allowances are ¼″ unless otherwise noted.

1. Create half-square triangles (refer to Half-Square Triangle Background, page 32) from the black and white squares.

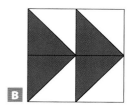

2. Sew sets of 2 blocks together to create Flying Geese. **A**

3. Sew Geese blocks together to create borders, noting numbers of Geese blocks in chart. **B**

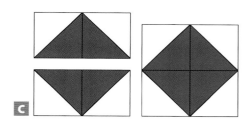

4. Sew sets of Geese blocks together for the 4 corner blocks. **C**

5. Piece together the blocks to form the horizontal and vertical borders. **D**

D Assemble borders. This is the layout for the baby-, lap-, and twin-sized quilts.

Make the Fox

1. Remove the fox pattern from the pattern pullout and tape it to your table.

2. Place the interfacing on top of the pattern and tape it in place.

3. Using chalk (or another marking tool), trace the fox onto the interfacing. Be sure the line is dark enough to show through the back of the interfacing.

4. Remove the interfacing. Place the accent fabric (with the fusible web already applied) over the cheeks, then ears, then tail of the pattern; trace the shapes; and cut them out. Set them aside. Do the same for the nose and eyes, using the black fabric with fusible web already applied.

5. Remove the tape and pattern, and place the interfacing on an ironing board or protected table. Begin collaging the fabric (see Creating the Collage, page 26). Don't worry if fabric goes outside the lines; you will cut out the fox. Press the collage as you complete each section.

6. After the collage is finished, place the accent pieces, nose, and eyes in position, and press.

7. Flip over the interfacing and cut out the fox on the drawn line.

8. Topstitch the fox using clear polyester thread (see Stitching the Collage to the Quilt Top, page 34). Press the finished fox.

9. Place the fox in the center of the pressed background fabric. Be sure the fox is completely flat and smoothed out, and pin it in place.

10. Thread your machine with the orange thread. Embroider around all the edges you traced from the pattern. Satin stitch works well, or you can use any other stitch you like.

11. Pin the vertical borders to the quilt top, matching centers. Sew the borders, and press the seam toward the borders. Sew the corner squares to the horizontal borders and press the seams toward the borders. Then sew these borders to the quilt top and press as you did for the first borders.

Finish

Refer to Finishing the Quilt (page 37) as needed.

Finish the quilt as desired.

I used a concentric circle quilting pattern for the background to contrast with the sharp lines in the border. I echo quilted the triangles in the black Geese and quilted a jagged, broken-glass pattern in the fox.

Scrappy Bits Appliqué

Windy Poplar

size shown: 50″ × 64″ (lap size)

To say that I love trees would be trite and a wild understatement. There is nothing more beautiful to me than tangled, gnarled, hopeful, stretching branches. I frequently stifle the urge to steal away into them. So naturally, when dreaming up quilts, I perpetually sketch trees. The title of this quilt refers to a book in one of my very favorite series, *Anne of Green Gables*.

MATERIALS	Baby/wall 40″ × 52″	Lap 50″ × 64″	Twin 62″ × 88″	Full/queen 86″ × 93″	King 104″ × 93″
Beige background	1⅝ yards	2⅝ yards	3⅞ yards	7¼ yards	7⅞ yards
Various green fabrics	1 yard total	1 yard total	1½ yards total	2 yards total	2½ yards total
Fusible web	2 yards	2 yards	3 yards	4 yards	5 yards
Backing	2¾ yards	3¼ yards	5½ yards	7⅞ yards	8⅝ yards
Batting	48″ × 60″	58″ × 72″	70″ × 96″	94″ × 101″	112″ × 101″
Binding	½ yard	⅝ yard	¾ yard	⅞ yard	1 yard
Lightweight, nonfusible interfacing	30″ × 45″	30″ × 45″	42″ × 65″	49″ × 75″	55″ × 85″
Windy Poplar pattern (on pullout page P1)	As is	As is	Enlarge 150%.	Enlarge 175%.	Enlarge 200%.

Additional supplies

- **Thread:** clear polyester, green, white

CUTTING

WOF = width of fabric

	Baby/wall	Lap	Twin	Full/queen	King
Background	40″ × 52″	40″ × 54″	40″ × 66″	Cut 3 panels 86″ × WOF. Piece along the 86″ sides. Cut to 86″ × 93″.	Cut 3 panels 93″ × WOF. Piece along the 93″ sides. Cut to 104″ × 93″.
Border (same fabric as background)	None	Cut 6 strips 5½″ × WOF.	Cut 6 strips 11½″ × WOF.	None	None
Backing	Cut 2 panels 48″ × WOF. Piece along the 48″ sides. Cut to 48″ × 60″.	Cut 2 panels 58″ × WOF. Piece along the 58″ sides. Cut to 58″ × 72″.	Cut 2 panels 96″ × WOF. Piece along the 96″ sides. Cut to 70″ × 96″.	Cut 3 panels 94″ × WOF. Piece along the 94″ sides. Cut to 94″ × 101″.	Cut 3 panels 101″ × WOF. Piece along the 101″ sides. Cut to 112″ × 101″.
Binding (page 44)	Cut 5 strips 2½″ × WOF.	Cut 7 strips 2½″ × WOF.	Cut 9 strips 2½″ × WOF.	Cut 10 strips 2½″ × WOF.	Cut 11 strips 2½″ × WOF.

Prepare the Collage Fabric

Refer to Preparing the Collage Fabric (page 22).

1. Apply fusible web to the back of the green collage fabric (see Applying Fusible Web, page 25).

2. After the web is applied, remove the paper and cut the green fabric using the wood grain technique in Cutting the Fabric (page 25).

Make the Tree

1. Remove the tree pattern from the pattern pullout and tape it to your table.

2. Place the interfacing on top of the template pattern, and tape it in place.

3. Using chalk (or another marking tool), trace the tree onto the interfacing. Be sure the line is dark enough to show through the back of the interfacing. You can extend the lines of the trunk if you want a taller tree.

4. Remove the tape and pattern, and place the interfacing on an ironing board or protected table. Begin collaging the fabric (see Creating the Collage, page 26). Do not worry if fabric goes outside the lines; you will cut out the tree. Press the collage as you complete each section.

5. After the collage is finished and pressed securely in place, flip the interfacing over and cut out the tree along the drawn line, using scissors or a rotary cutter. Place aside.

6. Spread the background fabric on a table or the floor. Smooth out completely, and tape in place as if basting.

7. Place the tree in the center of the secured background fabric. Be sure the tree is completely flat and smoothed out, and then pin it in place.

8. Topstitch the tree using clear thread (see Stitching the Collage to the Quilt Top, page 34). Press when finished.

9. Thread your machine with the green thread. Embroider around the edges using a satin stitch.

Finish

Refer to Finishing the Quilt (page 37) as needed to add the borders to the lap- and twin-sized quilts.

Finish the quilt as desired.

I used a wood grain quilting pattern in the tree and a meandering back-and-forth design for the background.

Scrappy Bits Appliqué

Blocks for Elephants

size shown: 54½″ × 66½″ (lap size)

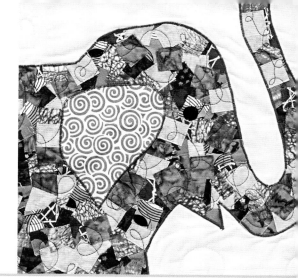

I originally made *Blocks for Elephants* for a good friend who was having her fourth baby girl. I knew she loved elephants, and I had some gorgeous purple batiks that I was aching to use. That has always been one of my favorite quilts, maybe because the incredible batiks were such a delight to work with. For this design, I wanted the blocks and the collage to engage with one another, so I positioned the blocks as though they are being shot out of the elephant's trunk.

MATERIALS	Baby/wall 36½″ × 44½″	Lap 54½″ × 66½″	Twin 72½″ × 88½″	Full/queen 81½″ × 99½″	King 108½″ × 96½″
Yellow fabrics	⅜ yard each of 6 different fabrics	½ yard each of 6 different fabrics	¾ yard each of 6 different fabrics	⅞ yard each of 6 different fabrics	1⅛ yards each of 6 different fabrics
White fabrics	1 yard	1¾ yards	3¼ yards	3½ yards	4¼ yards
Various purple fabric	¾ yard total	¾ yard total	1¼ yards total	1½ yards total	2½ yards total
Fusible web	1½ yards	1½ yards	2½ yards	3 yards	5 yards
Backing	2½ yards	3½ yards	5½ yards	7½ yards	8¾ yards
Batting	44″ × 52″	62″ × 74″	80″ × 96″	89″ × 107″	116″ × 104″
Binding	½ yard	⅝ yard	¾ yard	⅞ yard	1 yard
Quilter's Grid (if using the Quick Squares piecing method, page 30)	40½″ × 49½″	58½″ × 71½″	76½″ × 93½″	85½″ × 104½″	112½″ × 100″
Lightweight, nonfusible interfacing	19″ × 16″	27″ × 22″	34″ × 28″	38″ × 31″	49″ × 40″
Elephant pattern (on pullout page P1)	As is for a large elephant or reduce 66% for same proportions as shown.	As is	Enlarge 133%.	Enlarge 150%.	Enlarge 200%.

CUTTING

WOF = width of fabric

	Baby/wall	Lap	Twin	Full/queen	King*
Yellow	Cut 10 squares 4½″ × 4½″ of each of the 6 fabrics.	Cut 10 squares 6½″ × 6½″ of each of the 6 fabrics.	Cut 10 squares 8½″ × 8½″ of each of the 6 fabrics.	Cut 10 squares 9½″ × 9½″ of each of the 6 fabrics.	Cut 8 squares 12½″ × 12½″ of each of the 6 fabrics.
White	Cut 50 squares 4½″ × 4½″.	Cut 50 squares 6½″ × 6½″.	Cut 50 squares 8½″ × 8½″.	Cut 50 squares 9½″ × 9½″.	Cut 36 squares 12½″ × 12½″.
Backing	Cut 2 panels 44″ × WOF and piece along the 44″ sides. Cut to 44″ × 52″.	Cut 2 panels 62″ × WOF and piece along the 62″ sides. Cut to 62″ × 74″.	Cut 2 panels 96″ × WOF and piece along the 96″ sides. Cut to 80″ × 96″.	Cut 3 panels 89″ × WOF and piece along the 89″ sides. Cut to 89″ × 107″.	Cut 3 panels 104″ × WOF and piece along the 104″ sides. Cut to 116″ × 104″.
Binding (page 44)	Cut 5 strips 2½″ × WOF.	Cut 7 strips 2½″ × WOF.	Cut 9 strips 2½″ × WOF.	Cut 10 strips 2½″ × WOF.	Cut 11 strips 2½″ × WOF.

* For a king-size quilt, omit the top row and the bottom 2 rows in the design. The quilt will be 9 blocks wide and 8 blocks long. Be sure to arrange the background correctly before sewing on the elephant.

Prepare the Collage Fabric

Refer to Preparing the Collage Fabric (page 22).

1. Apply fusible web to the back of the purple and accent fabric (see Applying Fusible Web, page 25).

2. After the web is applied, remove the paper and cut the purple fabric using the desired cutting pattern. I used 1″ squares. See Cutting the Fabric (page 25). *Do not cut the accent fabric.*

3. Apply fusible web to a scrap of black fabric for the eye.

Make the Background

All seam allowances are ¼″ unless otherwise noted.

1. Arrange the squares according to the diagram, or to your liking. There will be extra squares.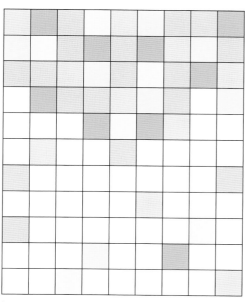

2. Piece the squares together either by using the technique in Quick Pieced Backgrounds (page 30) or by traditional means.

A Arrange squares.

Make the Elephant

1. Remove the elephant pattern from the pattern pullout and tape it to your table.

2. Place the interfacing on top of the template pattern, and tape it in place.

3. Using chalk (or another marking tool), trace the elephant onto the interfacing. Be sure the line is dark enough to show through the fabric.

4. Remove the interfacing. Place the accent fabric (with the fusible web already applied) over the ear on the pattern, trace, and then cut out. Set aside. Do the same for the eye, using the black fabric with fusible web already applied.

5. Remove the tape and pattern, and place the interfacing on an ironing board or protected table. Begin collaging the fabric (see Creating the Collage, page 26). Do not worry if fabric goes outside the lines; you will cut out the elephant. Press the collage as you complete each section.

6. After the collage is finished, place the accent pieces, ear and eye, in position and press.

7. Flip the interfacing over and cut out the elephant on the drawn line.

8. Topstitch the elephant using clear thread (see Stitching the Collage to the Quilt Top, page 34). Press the finished elephant.

9. Place the elephant in the correct position on the pressed background fabric. Be sure the elephant is completely flat and smoothed out, and pin it in place.

10. Thread your machine with the purple thread. Embroider around all the edges you traced from the pattern. I used a satin stitch.

Finish

Refer to Finishing the Quilt (page 37) as needed.

Finish the quilt as desired.

I wanted to create a lot of movement with the quilting stitches, so I quilted wild curls that branch off from one another, starting at the trunk and then moving up and out, like water shooting from an elephant's trunk.

Stormy Quilt

size shown: 50″ × 64″ (lap size)

I do love a good thunderstorm. A cozy evening in with a roaring tempest outside might be one of my very favorite things. This would be a fun quilt for kids and adults alike.

MATERIALS	Baby/wall 40″ × 52″	Lap 50″ × 64″	Twin 62″ × 88″	Full/queen 86″ × 93″	King 104″ × 93″
Background	1⅝ yards	2⅝ yards	3⅞ yards	7¼ yards	7⅞ yards
Various gray fabrics	1 yard total	1 yard total	1½ yards total	1¾ yards total	2 yards total
Various yellow fabrics	1 yard total	1 yard total	1½ yards total	1¾ yards total	2 yards total
Fusible web	4 yards	4 yards	6 yards	7 yards	8 yards
Backing	2¾ yards	3¼ yards	5½ yards	7⅞ yards	8⅝ yards
Batting	48″ × 60″	58″ × 72″	70″ × 96″	94″ × 101″	112″ × 101″
Binding	½ yard	⅝ yard	¾ yard	⅞ yard	1 yard
Lightweight, nonfusible interfacing	29″ × 45″	29″ × 45″	42″ × 65″	48″ × 77″	61″ × 85″
Stormy patterns (on pullout pages P1 and P2)	As is	As is	Enlarge 150%.	Enlarge 175%.	Enlarge 200%.

Additional supplies

- Small blue fabric scraps for raindrops
- **Thread:** clear polyester, white, yellow

CUTTING

WOF = width of fabric

	Baby/wall	Lap	Twin	Full/queen	King
Background	40″ × 52″	40″ × 54″	40″ × 66″	Cut 3 panels 86″ × WOF. Piece along the 86″ sides. Cut to 86″ × 93″.	Cut 3 panels 93″ × WOF. Piece along the 93″ sides. Cut to 104″ × 93″.
Border (same fabric as background)	None	Cut 6 strips 5½″ × WOF.	Cut 6 strips 11½″ × WOF.	None	None
Backing	Cut 2 panels 48″ × WOF; Piece along the 48″ sides. Cut to 48″ × 60″.	Cut 2 panels 58″ × WOF; Piece along the 58″ sides. Cut to 58″ × 72″.	Cut 2 panels 96″ × WOF. Piece along the 96″ sides. Cut to 70″ × 96″.	Cut 3 panels 94″ × WOF. Piece along the 94″ sides. Cut to 94″ × 101″.	Cut 3 panels 101″ × WOF. Piece along the 101″ sides. Cut to 112″ × 101″.
Binding (page 44)	Cut 5 strips 2½″ × WOF.	Cut 7 strips 2½″ × WOF.	Cut 9 strips 2½″ × WOF.	Cut 10 strips 2½″ × WOF.	Cut 11 strips 2½″ × WOF.

Prepare the Collage Fabric

Refer to Preparing the Collage Fabric (page 22).

1. Apply fusible web to the back of the gray and yellow collage fabric as well as 3 scraps of blue fabric (see Applying Fusible Web, page 25).

2. After the web is applied, remove the paper and cut the gray and yellow fabric using the mosaic cutting technique in Cutting the Fabric (page 25).

Brew Up a Storm!

1. Remove the cloud, 4 lightning bolts, and the raindrop pattern sheets from the pattern pullout and tape them to your table.

2. Place the interfacing on top of the template patterns, and tape it in place.

3. Using chalk (or another marking tool), trace the cloud onto the interfacing. Be sure the line is dark enough to show through the back of the interfacing. Remove the tape and pattern.

4. Likewise, trace 7 lightning bolts onto interfacing.

5. Trace the raindrop 3 times onto a scrap of interfacing. Then trace it onto the 3 different pieces of blue fabric with fusible web on the back.

6. Place the interfacing on an ironing board or protected table. Begin collaging the gray fabric on the cloud (see Creating the Collage, page 26). Do not worry if fabric goes outside the lines; you will cut out the cloud. Press the collage as you complete each section.

7. After the collage is finished and pressed securely in place, flip the interfacing over and cut out the cloud along the drawn line, using scissors or a rotary cutter. Place aside.

8. Repeat Steps 5 and 6 for the lightning bolts using the yellow fabric.

9. Topstitch the cloud and lightning bolts using clear thread (see Stitching the Collage to the Quilt Top, page 34). Press when finished.

10. Spread the background fabric on the table. Smooth out completely and tape in place, as if basting (use the floor if needed).

11. Place the cloud and lightning bolts in the desired locations on the secured background

fabric. Be sure they are completely flat and smoothed out, and pin them in place.

12. Thread your machine with the white thread. Embroider around the edges of the cloud using a satin stitch. Repeat with yellow for the bolts. Put raindrops in place, press, and then embroider with blue thread.

Finish

Refer to Finishing the Quilt (page 37) as needed to add the borders to the lap and twin sizes.

Finish the quilt as desired.

I used a sharp, broken glass–like pattern for the background, throwing in some quilted lightning bolts. In the cloud I quilted simple, swirly lines.

Scrappy Bits Appliqué

Around the World

size shown: 43″ × 28″ (baby/wall size)

My perpetual wanderlust inspired this quilt. It looks perfect in a kid's room, master bedroom, living room, office … any room, really.

MATERIALS	Baby/wall 43″ × 28″	Lap 66″ × 47″	Twin 89″ × 62″	Full/queen 94″ × 88″	King 106″ × 94″
Background fabric	¾ yard	1⅜ yards	2 yards	2½ yards	2½ yards
Various blue fabrics	½ yard total	⅝ yard total	⅞ yard total	1 yard total	1 yard total
Various orange fabrics	½ yard total	⅝ yard total	⅞ yard total	1 yard total	1 yard total
Various green fabrics	½ yard total	⅝ yard total	⅞ yard total	1 yard total	1 yard total
Fusible web	3 yards	3¾ yards	5¼ yards	6 yards	6 yards
White border	½ yard	1⅝ yards	3 yards	4⅜ yards	5¼ yards
Backing	1½ yards	3¼ yards	5½ yards	8⅛ yards	8⅝ yards
Hanging sleeve fabric	½ yard	½ yard	¾ yard	¾ yard	¾ yard
Batting	51″ × 36″	74″ × 55″	97″ × 70″	102″ × 96″	114″ × 102″
Binding	⅜ yard	⅝ yard	¾ yard	⅞ yard	⅞ yard
Lightweight, nonfusible interfacing	37″ × 26″	45″ × 31″	62″ × 42″	70″ × 48″	70″ × 48″
Around the World pattern (on pullout page P2)	As is	Enlarge 125%.	Enlarge 175%.	Enlarge 200%.	Enlarge 200%.

Additional supplies
- **Gluestick** (I prefer Elmer's)
- **Thread:** clear polyester, white

CUTTING
WOF = width of fabric

	Baby/wall	Lap	Twin	Full/queen	King
Background	37″ × 22″	46″ × 27″	65″ × 38″	Cut 2 panels 44″ × WOF and piece along the 44″ sides. Cut to 70″ × 44″.	Cut 2 panels 44″ × WOF and piece along the 44″ sides. Cut to 74″ × 44″.
Border	Cut 4 strips 3½″ × WOF.	Cut 5 strips 10½″ × WOF.	Cut 8 strips 12½″ × WOF.	Cut 4 strips 22½″ × WOF and 5 strips 12½″ × WOF.	Cut 4 strips 25½″ × WOF and 5 strips 16½″ × WOF.
Backing	51″ × 36″	Cut 2 panels 55″ × WOF and piece along the 55″ sides. Cut to 74″ × 55″.	Cut 2 panels 97″ × WOF and piece along the 97″ sides. Cut to 97″ × 70″.	Cut 3 panels 96″ × WOF and piece along the 96″ sides. Cut to 102″ × 96″.	Cut 3 panels 102″ × WOF and piece along the 102″ sides. Cut to 114″ × 102″.
Binding (page 44)	Cut 4 strips 2½″ × WOF.	Cut 7 strips 2½″ × WOF.	Cut 9 strips 2½″ × WOF.	Cut 10 strips 2½″ × WOF.	Cut 11 strips 2½″ × WOF.
Hanging sleeve (page 48), if needed	9″ × 43″	9″ × 66″	9″ × 89″	9″ × 94″	9″ × 106″

Prepare the Collage Fabric

Refer to Preparing the Collage Fabric (page 22).

1. Apply fusible web to the back of the blue, green, and orange collage fabric (see Applying Fusible Web, page 25).

2. After the web is applied, remove the paper and cut the fabric using the random mosaic technique in Cutting the Fabric (page 25).

Make the Map

All seam allowances are ¼″ unless otherwise noted.

1. Remove the map pattern sheets from the pattern pullout and tape the pattern to your table.

2. Place the interfacing on top of the template pattern, and tape it in place.

3. Using dark chalk (or another marking tool), trace the map onto the interfacing. *Be sure the line is dark enough to show through the back of the interfacing.*

Tip *If you don't feel like including every single island—then don't! If you want to be able to put this quilt in the washing machine, I would recommend skipping the islands and only including the continents, because the tiny islands would likely get lost or shredded in the wash.*

4. Remove the tape and pattern, and place the interfacing on an ironing board or protected table. Begin collaging the fabric (see Creating the Collage, page 26). Do not worry if fabric goes outside the lines; you will cut out the pieces. Press the collage as you complete each section.

5. Place the collage aside. Tape the map template back on the table. Spread out the background fabric, centering it on top of the map pattern. Smooth it out completely and tape it in place, as if basting. The map template should be visible through the fabric.

6. Using sharp scissors, cut out the large pieces, a piece at a time. After cutting each piece, place it on the background fabric in its correct spot, making sure it is completely smoothed out, and then pin in place. I pinned each piece as I cut it out to avoid a mixed-up mess, particularly with the islands! Repeat for all the large pieces (pieces large enough to put a pin through).

Be sure to plan as you cut, so you don't end up getting confused and placing Iceland in Indonesia!

7. After all the large pieces are pinned in place, start cutting out an island at a time, and place each in the correct spot. After every few islands (or after each archipelago), glue the islands down with a gluestick. Regular Elmer's gluesticks are perfect for this because they secure the islands well and easily; the glue won't muck up your sewing machine, and it will wash out easily! Repeat for all of the islands.

8. After all of the pieces are cut out and secured well to the background fabric, topstitch the pieces using clear thread (see Stitching the Collage to the Quilt Top, page 34). I topstitched a continent (section) at a time, hitting all the islands as I got near them. You may go around the edges of the continents with a satin stitch if you want to prevent fraying or if you want to be able to wash the quilt in a washing machine. I did not for a few reasons: It would take a very long time, I do not plan to put this quilt in the washing machine, and I liked the exposed raw edges.

9. Use Fray Check on all raw edges to prevent any future fraying, especially around the edges of the continents and the islands. Be sure to test the Fray Check on a sample of the fabric first, as well as on any marks you've made, to be sure there won't be any bleeding through the fabric.

10. For the baby/wall quilt, sew the top and bottom borders to the quilt top, trimming to size, and then add the side borders. For the lap and twin sizes, piece the border pieces end to end, and then trim to size and add to the quilt top. For the full/queen and king sizes, piece the wider border strips and cut to size for the top and bottom borders, and then sew to the quilt top. Piece the narrower border strips end to end and cut to size for the side borders; then add to the quilt top (see Borders, page 37).

Finish

Refer to Finishing the Quilt (page 37) as needed.

Finish the quilt as desired, adding the optional hanging sleeve (page 48) if you wish.

I quilted around the continents to make them stand out, and then used a concentric circle quilting pattern on the background and border to contrast with the geometric pattern in the background and in the collage.

Branching Out

size shown: 55½″ × 72″ (lap size)

I can't stop myself from collaging trees. It's kind of a compulsion. This is a great project for experienced quilters and beginners alike. The pieced background is a very simple, straight-forward pattern and would even look lovely as a stand-alone quilt. The branch can, of course, be done on a solid background as well. I've made several versions of this design as wallhangings with solid backgrounds, which have proven to be great, quick gifts!

MATERIALS	Baby/wall 35½″ × 46″	Lap 55½″ × 72″	Twin 65½″ × 85″	Full/queen 85½″ × 94″	King 105½″ × 105½″
Dark shades of turquoise fabric	⅜ yard each of 2 different fabrics	½ yard each of 2 different fabrics	⅝ yard each of 2 different fabrics	¾ yard each of 2 different fabrics	1⅛ yards each of 2 different fabrics
Medium shades of turquoise fabric	⅜ yard each of 2 different fabrics	¾ yard each of 2 different fabrics	¾ yard each of 2 different fabrics	1 yard each of 2 different fabrics	1⅛ yards each of 2 different fabrics
Light shades of turquoise fabric	⅝ yard each of 2 different fabrics	1⅛ yards each of 2 different fabrics	1⅜ yards each of 2 different fabrics	2 yards each of 2 different fabrics	2¾ yards each of 2 different fabrics
Gray fabric (for blocks)	¼ yard each of 2 different fabrics	½ yard each of 2 different fabrics	⅝ yard each of 2 different fabrics	¾ yard each of 2 different fabrics	⅞ yard each of 2 different fabrics
White	½ yard	⅞ yard	1 yard	1½ yards	2⅜ yards
Various gray fabrics (for branch)	¾ yard total	1 yard total	1⅛ yards total	1⅜ yards total	2 yards total
Yellow fabric	⅛ yard	⅛ yard	¼ yard	¼ yard	¼ yard
Fusible web	1¾ yards	2¼ yards	2⅜ yards	3¼ yards	4½ yards
Quilter's Grid (if using the Half-Square Triangle piecing method, page 32)	45″ × 59″	65″ × 85″	75″ × 98″	95″ × 105″	115″ × 115″
Batting	43″ × 54″	63″ × 80″	73″ × 93″	93″ × 102″	113″ × 113″

Materials continued on next page.

MATERIALS	Baby/wall 35½″ × 46″	Lap 55½″ × 72″	Twin 65½″ × 85″	Full/queen 85½″ × 94″	King 105½″ × 105½″
Backing	2½ yards	3½ yards	5¼ yards	7¾ yards	9½ yards
Binding	½ yard	⅝ yard	¾ yard	⅞ yard	1 yard
Lightweight, nonfusible interfacing	38″ × 16″	55″ × 22″	63″ × 25″	71″ × 28″	88″ × 34″
Branch pattern (on pullout pages P1 and P2)	As is for a large branch, or reduce 66%.	As is	Enlarge 116%.	Enlarge 133%.	Enlarge 166%.

Additional supplies

- Scraps of gray and white fabric for the wings and beaks

- **Thread:** clear, purple, and white

CUTTING

WOF = width of fabric

	Baby/wall	Lap	Twin	Full/queen*	King**
Color 1— dark turquoise	10 squares 4½″ × 4½″	10 squares 6½″ × 6½″	10 squares 7½″ × 7½″	8 squares 9½″ × 9½″	7 squares 11½″ × 11½″
Color 2— dark turquoise	8 squares 4½″ × 4½″	8 squares 6½″ × 6½″	8 squares 7½″ × 7½″	7 squares 9½″ × 9½″	6 squares 11½″ × 11½″
Color 3— gray	8 squares 4½″ × 4½″	8 squares 6½″ × 6½″	8 squares 7½″ × 7½″	6 squares 9½″ × 9½″	6 squares 11½″ × 11½″
Color 4— gray	8 squares 4½″ × 4½″	8 squares 6½″ × 6½″	8 squares 7½″ × 7½″	6 squares 9½″ × 9½″	5 squares 11½″ × 11½″
Color 5— medium turquoise	13 squares 4½″ × 4½″	13 squares 6½″ × 6½″	13 squares 7½″ × 7½″	10 squares 9½″ × 9½″	9 squares 11½″ × 11½″
Color 6— medium turquoise	13 squares 4½″ × 4½″	13 squares 6½″ × 6½″	13 squares 7½″ × 7½″	11 squares 9½″ × 9½″	9 squares 11½″ × 11½″
Color 7— light turquoise	21 squares 4½″ × 4½″	21 squares 6½″ × 6½″	21 squares 7½″ × 7½″	15 squares 9½″ × 9½″	14 squares 11½″ × 11½″
Color 8— light turquoise	29 squares 4½″ × 4½″	29 squares 6½″ × 6½″	29 squares 7½″ × 7½″	27 squares 9½″ × 9½″	24 squares 11½″ × 11½″
Color 9— white	10 squares 4½″ × 4½″ and 10 squares 4″ × 4″	10 squares 6½″ × 6½″ and 10 squares 6″ × 6″	10 squares 7½″ × 7½″ and 10 squares 7″ × 7″	10 squares 9½″ × 9½″ and 10 squares 9″ × 9″	10 squares 11½″ × 11½″ and 10 squares 11″ × 11″
Backing	Cut 2 panels 43″ × WOF and piece along the 43″ sides. Cut to 43″ × 54″.	Cut 2 panels 63″ × WOF and piece along the 63″ sides. Cut to 63″ × 80″.	Cut 2 panels 93″ × WOF and piece along the 93″ sides. Cut to 73″ × 93″.	Cut 3 panels 93″ × WOF and piece along the 93″ sides. Cut to 93″ × 102″.	Cut 3 panels 113″ × WOF and piece along the 113″ sides. Cut to 113″ × 113″.
Binding (page 44)	Cut 5 strips 2½″ × WOF.	Cut 7 strips 2½″ × WOF.	Cut 9 strips 2½″ × WOF.	Cut 10 strips 2½″ × WOF.	Cut 12 strips 2½″ × WOF.

* For a full/queen-size quilt, omit the top 2 rows from the design. The quilt will be 10 blocks wide and 11 blocks long.

** For a king-size quilt, omit the top 3 rows from the design. The quilt will be 10 blocks wide and 10 blocks long.

Prepare the Collage Fabric

Refer to Preparing the Collage Fabric (page 22).

1. Apply fusible web to the back of the gray fabric, as well as the pieces of the yellow and white fabric for the birds (see Applying Fusible Web, page 25).

2. Make a copy of the bird from the pattern pullout at the back of the book. Cut out the circle to use as a template. Using chalk or a marking pencil, trace 2 circles onto the yellow scrap fabric and cut out. Do not remove the paper.

3. Cut the triangle wing template and trace 2 triangle wings onto a piece of the gray fabric. Remove the paper from the gray triangles.

4. Place the gray triangles on the yellow circles and press. After pressing, you may remove the paper from the yellow circles.

5. Use the beak template to trace 2 beaks on the white fabric. Cut out, and then remove the paper.

6. Remove the paper from the gray fabric and cut using the wood grain technique in Cutting the Fabric (page 25).

Piece the Background

Refer to Half-Square Triangle Background, page 32, as needed.

All seam allowances are ¼" unless otherwise noted.

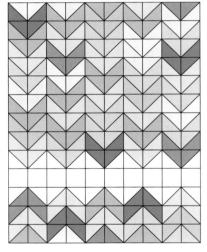

1. Make the half-square triangles. Refer to the diagram to see which colors to piece together, using the larger white squares for the half-square triangles. I suggest pinning all of the squares first and stacking them in order, then sewing, cutting, pressing, and trimming all in order as well, to avoid confusion.

2. Piece together the quilt top using fusible interfacing, or piece in the traditional manner, adding the solid row of smaller white squares as shown in the diagram.

3. Press seams in opposite directions where possible to help match the corners.

Build the Branches

1. Remove the branch pattern sheet from the pattern pullout and tape the pattern to your table. Note that the branch is in 4 pieces and continues at the dotted lines.

2. Place the interfacing on top of the pattern, and tape it in place.

3. Using chalk (or another marking tool), trace the branch onto the interfacing, moving the pattern or interfacing as necessary to trace the full image. Be sure the line is dark enough to show through the back of the interfacing.

4. Remove the tape and pattern, and place the interfacing on an ironing board or protected table. Begin collaging the fabric (see Creating the Collage, page 26). Do not worry if fabric goes outside the lines; you will cut out the branch. Press the collage as you complete each section.

5. After the collage is finished and pressed securely in place, flip the interfacing over and cut out the branch along the drawn line, using scissors or a rotary cutter.

6. Topstitch the branch using clear thread (see Stitching the Collage to the Quilt Top, page 34). Press when finished.

7. Spread the background fabric on a table or the floor. Smooth out completely and tape in place as if basting.

8. Place the branch centered between the white row and the top of the quilt, and pin it in place. Be sure the branch is completely flat and smoothed out.

9. Thread your machine with the gray thread. Embroider around the edges using a satin stitch.

10. Place the birds on the desired branches and press to secure in place. Place and press their beaks. Embroider around the wings with the gray thread and around the bodies and beaks with white thread.

Finish

Refer to Finishing the Quilt (page 37) as needed.

Finish the quilt as desired.

- - - - - - - - - - - - - - - - - -

I chose a wavy triangular pattern to cover the whole quilt, to both complement and contrast with the pieced triangles.

Mini-Mosaic Trees

size shown: 20″ × 20″ (small wall size)

Another tree? Yes, yes. It can't be helped. I used this pattern in one of the very first raw-edge appliqué quilts I made. I love it on a solid or textured solid background, really allowing the collaged fabrics to tell the story.

MATERIALS	Small wall 20″ × 20″	Baby / large wall 40″ × 40″	Lap 60″ × 60″	Twin* 62″ × 82″	Full/queen 90″ × 90″	King 100″ × 100″
Background	⅝ yard	1¼ yards	3½ yards	4⅝ yards	7⅝ yards	8½ yards
Various blue, purple, and apricot fabrics	¾ yard total	1½ yards total	2¼ yards total	2⅜ yards total	3½ yards total	3¾ yards total
Fusible web	1½ yards	3 yards	4½ yards	4½ yards	7 yards	7½ yards
Backing	⅞ yard	2¾ yards	3⅞ yards	5⅛ yards	8¼ yards	9⅛ yards
Hanging sleeve fabric	⅜ yard	⅜ yard	⅝ yard	⅝ yard	⅞ yard	⅞ yard
Batting	28″ × 28″	48″ × 48″	68″ × 68″	70″ × 90″	98″ × 98″	108″ × 108″
Binding	⅜ yard	½ yard	⅝ yard	⅝ yard	⅞ yard	⅞ yard
Lightweight, non-fusible interfacing	25″ × 25″	45″ × 45″	64″ × 64″	66″ × 66″	94″ × 94″	104″ × 104″
Mini-Mosaic Trees patterns (pages 103–108)	As is	Enlarge 200%.	Enlarge 290%.	Enlarge 300%.	Enlarge 440%.	Enlarge 490%.

* For the twin size, you can center the tree vertically, or extend the trunk 20″. You will have enough collage fabric, and you can piece the additional interfacing from the areas on either side of the trunk.

CUTTING

WOF = width of fabric

	Small wall	Baby / large wall	Lap	Twin	Full/queen	King
Background	20″ × 20″	40″ × 40″	Cut 2 panels 60″ × WOF. Piece along the 60″ sides. Cut to 60″ × 60″.	Cut 2 panels 82″ × WOF. Piece along the 82″ sides. Cut to 62″ × 82″.	Cut 3 panels 90″ × WOF. Piece along the 90″ sides. Cut to 90″ × 90″.	Cut 3 panels 100″ × WOF. Piece along the 100″ sides. Cut to 100″ × 100″.
Backing	28″ × 28″	Cut 2 panels 48″ × WOF. Piece along the 48″ sides. Cut to 48″ × 48″.	Cut 2 panels 68″ × WOF. Piece along the 68″ sides. Cut to 68″ × 68″.	Cut 2 panels 90″ × WOF. Piece along the 90″ sides. Cut to 70″ × 90″.	Cut 3 panels 98″ × WOF. Piece along the 98″ sides. Cut to 98″ × 98″.	Cut 3 panels 108″ × WOF. Piece along the 108″ sides. Cut to 108″ × 108″.
Hanging sleeve (page 48), if needed	9″ × 20″	9″ × 40″	Cut 2 strips 9″ × WOF. Piece together and trim to 9″ × 60″.	Cut 2 strips 9″ × WOF. Piece together and trim to 9″ × 62″.	Cut 3 strips 9″ × WOF. Piece together and trim to 9″ × 90″.	Cut 3 strips 9″ × WOF. Piece together and trim to 9″ × 100″.
Binding (page 44)	Cut 3 strips 2½″ × WOF.	Cut 5 strips 2½″ × WOF.	Cut 7 strips 2½″ × WOF.	Cut 8 strips 2½″ × WOF.	Cut 11 strips 2½″ × WOF.	Cut 11 strips 2½″ × WOF.

Prepare the Collage Fabric

Refer to Preparing the Collage Fabric, page 22.

1. Apply fusible web to the back of the collage fabric (see Applying Fusible Web, page 25).

2. After the web is applied, remove the paper and cut the fabric using the mosaic technique in Cutting the Fabric (page 25).

Let's Collage!

1. Place the interfacing on top of each page of the Mini-Mosaic Trees patterns (pages 103–108) and tape it in place.

2. Using chalk (or another marking tool), trace each section of the tree onto the interfacing. Be sure the line is dark enough to show through the back of the interfacing. You can extend the trunk lines if you want a taller tree.

3. Remove the tape and pattern, and place the interfacing on an ironing board or protected table. Begin collaging the fabric (see Creating the Collage, page 26). Do not worry if fabric goes outside the lines; you will be cutting out the tree. Press the collage as you complete each section.

4. Once the collage is finished and pressed securely in place, flip the interfacing over and cut out the tree along the drawn line, using scissors or a rotary cutter. Set aside.

5. Spread the background fabric on the table or the floor. Smooth out completely and tape in place.

6. Spray the back of the tree with temporary adhesive (or basting) spray. Place in the center of the background and smooth in place. If any branches come loose, use a gluestick to secure them in place. If you do not want to use adhesives, you may pin in place. Be sure the tree is completely flat and smoothed out.

7. I chose to quilt these wallhangings in a straight-line quilting pattern with the rows less than ¼″ apart. Since the quilting is so dense, I was able to skip the topstitching step, allowing the quilt stitches to secure the collage in place.

If you choose a looser quilting pattern, be sure to topstitch the collage (page 34) before basting.

Finish

Refer to Finishing the Quilt (page 37) as needed.

Finish the quilt as desired, adding the optional hanging sleeve (page 48) if you wish.

Fallen Leaves Throw Pillows

size shown: 16″ × 16″

This is a fun and quick project, perfect for those who want to try out the style but maybe don't want to start with a whole quilt. The pillows would pair perfectly with many of the quilt patterns in this book. This project makes both pillows.

MATERIALS

Makes 2 pillows.

- **Background:** 1 yard
- **Back of pillows:** 1 yard
- **Backing (will be on the inside of the pillows):** 1⅜ yards
- **Various teal and green fabrics:** ½ yard total
- **Various orange and yellow fabrics:** ½ yard total
- **Fusible web:** 2 yards
- **Lightweight, nonfusible interfacing:** ½ yard

Additional supplies

- **Thread:** clear polyester, white, blue, orange
- **Zippers, 16″:** 2
- **Pillow forms, 16″ × 16″:** 2

CUTTING

For the pillows, you will have 4 panels: a front and a back for each of the 2 pillows. Rather than basting and quilting 4 different panels (which you can certainly do, if you prefer), I like to piece them all together so I only have to baste and quilt once.

Background
- Cut 1 piece 18″ × 36″.

Back of pillows
- Cut 1 piece 18″ × 36″.

Interfacing
- Cut 2 pieces 18″ × 18″.

Prepare the Pillow Top

1. Piece the background with the back-of-pillows fabric lengthwise (along the 36″ side). **A**

2. Draw a line with a marking tool down the center of the piece, perpendicular to the seam. **B**

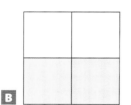

Prepare the Collage Fabric

Refer to Preparing the Collage Fabric (page 22).

1. Apply fusible web to the back of the orange, yellow, teal, and green fabric (see Applying Fusible Web, page 25).

2. After the web is applied, remove the paper and cut the fabric using the random mosaic technique in Cutting the Fabric (page 25).

Make the Pillows

1. Remove the 2 leaf patterns (pullout page P2) and tape them to your table.

2. Place the interfacing on top of the template patterns and tape it in place.

3. Using chalk (or another marking tool), trace the leaves onto the interfacing.

4. Remove the tape and pattern, and place the interfacing on an ironing board or protected table. Begin collaging the fabric (see Creating the Collage, page 26). Do not worry if fabric goes outside the lines; you will cut out the leaves. Press the collage as you complete each section.

5. Topstitch the leaves using clear thread (see Stitching the Collage to the Quilt Top, page 34).

6. Flip the interfacing over and cut out the leaves on the drawn line. Do not worry if you cut some stitches; all loose stitches will be caught when the leaves are appliquéd onto the background.

7. Place each leaf in the center of its panel. Be sure each leaf is completely flat and smoothed out, and then pin it in place.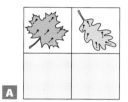

8. Embroider around all the edges of the leaves, using a satin stitch with thread that matches each leaf.

Quilt

Refer to Finishing the Quilt (page 37) as needed.

1. Baste the backing, batting, and pieced pillow fronts and backs.

2. Quilt as desired.

3. Cut along the seam between the leaves and the back of the pillow fabric, as well as along the line drawn down the center. You should have 4 equal panels. Trim each to a 16½″ square with the leaves centered.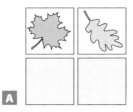

Install the Zipper

1. Place the right side of the zipper on the bottom edge of the right side of a leaf panel, and pin in place.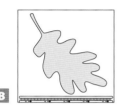

2. Using a zipper foot, sew the zipper to the panel with about a ¼″ seam allowance.

3. Line up the leaf panel with the back of the pillow, right sides together. Pin the right side of the zipper to the right side of the bottom edge of the pillow back. Sew the zipper to that panel.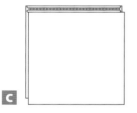

4. Press the seams away from the zipper.

Put Together the Pillow

1. With right sides facing, line up the 2 panels and pin in place. Unzip the zipper about halfway.

2. Sew around the 3 pinned sides with a ¼″ seam allowance. Trim the corners.

3. Unzip the zipper completely and turn the pillow cover right side out. Press the finished pillow cover.

4. Repeat for the other pillow.

5. Insert the pillow forms, gently filling the corners, and zip the covers closed.

I quilted the veins inside the leaves and whimsical swirls on the background to imply wind.

Gallery

Birds on a Branch

51˝ × 27˝

Here is another version of *Branching Out* (page 77).

Blue Ridge Mountains

36″ × 24″

I made this quilt for my mother-in-law, who lives in Virginia. I was inspired
by all the gushing my husband has done over the beauty and majesty of the
Blue Ridge Mountains. As you can see, the collage covers the whole quilt, and I used
different shapes to represent the different elements. I liked the way the unfinished edges
of the collage looked so much that I chose not to square it off and add binding.

Oh Deer

24″ × 36″

This piece sews up quickly and makes for a really fun wallhanging or gift.

Brontosaurus

34″ × 52″

A design like this is great as a baby quilt. Choose your colors and have fun.

Giraffe

37″ × 54″

This is another sweet, fast, and gender-neutral baby quilt.

Roots

20″ × 20″

This was one of the first pieces I made when I started playing with raw-edge appliqué.

Inverted Mosaic Tree

18″ × 19″

This is another way to use the Mini Mosaic Trees patterns (pages 103–108). I collaged the
background and used a solid piece of fabric for the tree.

The Kraken

40˝ × 58˝

I had a ton of fun making this fellow. I think if I make it again,
I will piece some squares into the background that look like air bubbles.

Use the following chart to determine the amount or fabric and batting to purchase when you are designing your own quilt.

Yardage is based on 40˝-wide fabric, unless otherwise noted.

Type	Mattress size	Suggested quilt size	Background fabric	Backing fabric*	Batting, packaged	Batting by the yard (90˝ wide)	Binding (2½˝ cut strips*)
Crib / child throw	28˝ × 52˝	36˝ × 54˝	1⅝ yards	2½ yards	45˝ × 60˝	1¼ yards (or 1¾ yards for 45˝ wide)	½ yard
Adult throw	n/a	50˝ × 60˝	2⅞ yards	3¼ yards	72˝ × 90˝	1⅝ yards	⅝ yard
Twin	39˝ × 75˝	63˝ × 87˝	4⅞ yards	5⅜ yards	81˝ × 96˝	2¾ yards	¾ yard
Long twin	39˝ × 80˝	63˝ × 92˝	5⅛ yards	5⅝ yards	120˝ × 120˝	2⅞ yards	¾ yard
Double	54˝ × 75˝	78˝ × 87˝	4⅞ yards	7¼ yards	90˝ × 108˝	2¾ yards	¾ yard
Queen	60˝ × 80˝	84˝ × 92˝	7 yards	7¾ yards	120˝ × 120˝	5⅛ yards	⅞ yard
King	78˝ × 80˝	102˝ × 92˝	7¾ yards	8⅜ yards	120˝ × 120˝	5⅝ yards	⅞ yard
California king	72˝ × 84˝	96˝ × 96˝	8 yards	8¾ yards	120˝ × 120˝	5⅞ yards	⅞ yard

* Backing dimensions are quilt dimensions plus 4˝ on each side.

Mini-Mosaic Trees Pattern

Scrappy Bits Appliqué

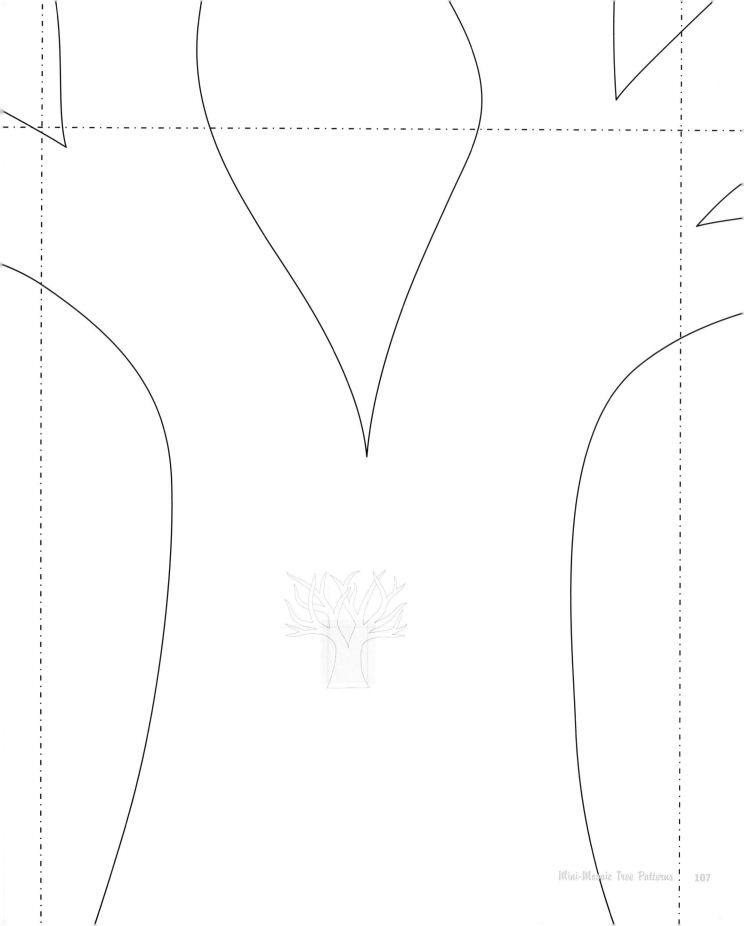

Scrappy Bits Appliqué

Resources

Fabric

Fabric used in the quilt projects was generously provided by the following companies. Their websites are great resources for looking at fabric and finding stores that sell the fabrics.

Timeless Treasures
Most of the monochromatic prints, solids, and batiks used in the collages are from Timeless Treasures, as well as several of the background fabrics. The company has a great collection of basics.
ttfabrics.com

Michael Miller Fabrics
A lot of the unique prints used in the collages and backings are from Michael Miller.
michaelmillerfabrics.com

Robert Kaufman Fabrics
I used Kona Cotton Solids, Quilter's Linen, and Quilter's Tussah for several of the backgrounds of the quilts in this book.
robertkaufman.com

Westminster Fabrics
I used several of Westminster's beautiful prints in my collages.
westminsterfabrics.com

Dear Stella
Several lovely Dear Stella prints appear in my collages as well.
dearstelladesign.com

Supplies

Warm Company
I love Warm Company batting. I used Warm & Natural batting for all of the quilts in this book.
warmcompany.com

Pellon
Pellon has a lot of great fusible webs, interfacing, and tracing cloths. I used its 725 Heavy-Duty Wonder-Under fusible web for all the collages in this book, as well as its 910 Sew-In Featherweight interfacing for all of the projects that require interfacing. Pellon also makes 820 Quilter's Grid and 821 Quilter's Grid On-Point fusible backing for square piecing, and 810 Tru-Grid for tracing and enlarging patterns.
pellonprojects.com

Oliso
Oliso has amazing irons. I use the Oliso Pro Smart Iron with iTouch Technology TG1600, and it is an absolute dream!
oliso.com

Superior Threads
I love Superior's MonoPoly monofilament thread. I used the same spool for all of the collages in this book, with a lot of thread left over!
superiorthread.com

Havel's Sewing
I used several pairs of Havel's incredible scissors for the projects in this book.
havelssewing.com

Prym Consumer (Dritz and Omnigrid)
Both Dritz and Omnigrid are outstanding brands with great products for quilting. I highly recommend the Omnigrid rotary cutters, rotary mats, and rulers, as well as the Dritz marking pens, binding clips, curved basting pins, and Fray Check.
www.prym-consumer-usa.com

Simplicity
Simplicity has a lot of great templates. I used several of its square templates in this book to cut the fabric for the pieced backgrounds and borders.
simplicity.com

Bottle Tree
My online fabric, pattern, and quilt kit shop.
thebottletree.net

About the author

Shannon Brinkley is a self-taught quilter and designer of modern quilt patterns. She studied education in college and holds two teaching certifications. A lifelong learner herself, Shannon has always loved sharing her knowledge and encouraging others to learn and try new things. She has been creating things with her hands since she was a very young girl, but fell madly in love with modern quilting in college. Shannon lives in Austin, Texas, with her always supportive and loving husband, Matt, and wonderfully creative son, Davin. See more of Shannon's quilts and patterns at thebottletree.net.

bottle tree

QUILTS ᐧ PATTERNS ᐧ FABRIC

stash BOOKS ®

fabric arts for a handmade lifestyle

If you're craving beautiful authenticity in a time of mass-production...Stash Books is for you. Stash Books is a line of how-to books celebrating fabric arts for a handmade lifestyle. Backed by C&T Publishing's solid reputation for quality, Stash Books will inspire you with contemporary designs, clear and simple instructions, and engaging photography.

www.stashbooks.com